Voyage to California
Written at Sea, 1852

The Journal of Lucy Kendall Herrick

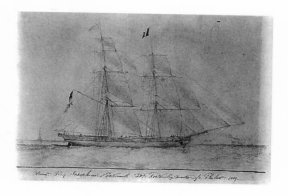

To Lucy's daughters, Lucy and Margaret Herrick,
without whom this book would never have been written

Voyage to California
Written at Sea, 1852

The Journal of Lucy Kendall Herrick

edited by Amy Requa Russell,
Marcia Russell Good, and Mary Good Lindgren

with an introduction by Andrew Rolle

HUNTINGTON LIBRARY
San Marino, California

Cover: Currier & Ives, *A Squall off Cape Horn*, undated. Museum of the City of New York, The Harry T. Peters Collection

Half-title page: Sketch of the *Josephine*. Courtesy, Peabody Essex Museum, Salem, Massachusetts

Page xi: *The William Paxton Family*. Courtesy, California Historical Society

Library of Congress Cataloging-in-Publication Data

Herrick, Lucy Kendall, 1828–1906

Voyage to California : written at sea, 1852 / Lucy Kendall Herrick and Amy Requa Russell ; edited and annotated by Marcia Russell Good and Mary Good Lindgren with an introduction by Andrew Rolle.

   p.   cm.

   ISBN 0-87328-165-9

   1. Herrick, Lucy Kendall, 1828–1906. 2. Josephine (Ship) 3. Voyages and travels. 4. Cape Horn (Chile) I. Russell, Amy Requa, 1896–1985. II. Good, Marcia Russell, 1924– . III. Lindgren, Mary Good. IV. Title.

G478.H47 1998

910.4′5--dc21   97-28146

CIP

HUNTINGTON LIBRARY PRESS

1151 Oxford Road • San Marino, CA 91108

CONTENTS

ILLUSTRATIONS

PREFACE

It was the journal "Written at Sea, 1852" by Lucy Fiennes Kendall that captured the hearts of my family back in the 1930s. Lucy was born in the Midlands of England in 1828, and was raised by her grandparents until she was nearly five. Her parents had sailed to New York to find a new life when she was only one and one-half years old. Upon returning to England for her daughter, Charlotte Kendall spent nearly a year regaining the child's affection before they could return to the father who had remained in New York. Lucy was to cross the Atlantic four more times before she, her mother, and her sister followed Joseph Kendall around the Horn to San Francisco. He was a "forty-niner" who had been bitten by "gold fever" when the news from California came to New York late in 1848.

Lucy's 1852 sea journal commands our greatest attention in this book. Enchantingly written, it describes the pursuits of passengers on calm days, the terror of terrible storms, the arbitrary discipline of the captain, a tragedy at sea, and at last, the longed-for docking in San Francisco.

Lucy wrote no more diaries after reaching San Francisco, but we have many family stories of those eventful days. It was not until after the birth of seven daughters and two sons that she wrote the memoirs of her early childhood in England—it is said she wrote it as a birthday gift for one of her daughters who undoubtedly had heard the story many times but now wanted it directly from her mother's pen.

In spite of pleas from her devoted relatives in England, Lucy had stayed in San Francisco, married, and raised a family. She and her husband, William Francis Herrick, passed on their artistic, creative, and loving traits to their children. The youngest, Florence, married Mark Requa and had three children. The eldest was my mother, Amy Requa Russell, the compiler of this book.

Two of Lucy's daughters, Margaret and Lucy, with a cousin, C. O. G. Miller, had researched family letters while preparing to publish the journal of their grandfather, Joseph Kendall (privately printed in 1935 under the title

A Landsman's Voyage to California*). *But it was the journal of his daughter Lucy, so full of unusual incidents of her perilous voyage, that inspired my mother to write the story of her maternal grandmother. Further research and communication between the Bay Area and Southern California produced much more of her story, and as Amy Russell set about collecting family stories, photos, letters, and books, she began to fill the gaps between Lucy's childhood memoirs, the journal of her voyage to California in 1852, and her later life in San Francisco.*

My mother was fascinated by the stories of her two grandmothers, both of whom had come to California very soon after the forty-niners. And, as I read Lucy's journal and then her childhood memoirs, I understood why my mother wanted to tell this story. The printing of this book is a fulfillment of her dream.

I am grateful for the help of my daughter, Mary Good Lindgren, for her many hours at the computer and her advice in editing. Professor Andrew Rolle, Research Scholar at the Huntington Library, who has written the Introduction, guided me in the early stages; he encouraged me to extend my researches and in the end to produce a more scholarly work. The late Terry Lee gave me support and encouragement when I most needed it.

Others who have helped are Stevey Bruce and her friend, Elizabeth Fleming Rhodes, who gave me advice about publishing; and Peggy Park Bernal and Kathleen Thorne-Thomsen of the Huntington Library Press.

Marcia Russell Good

The William Paxton family by Edward Williams; oil on canvas painted about 1825. Charlotte Paxton (Kendall) is seated at the left. (California Historical Society, gift of Amy Requa Russell.)

INTRODUCTION
By Andrew Rolle

On May 25, 1852, the good ship *Josephine* sailed out of New York Harbor past Sandy Hook, bound for California. She was a 947-ton freighter with forty-two persons aboard. In addition to her captain and crew members, she carried eight "cabin passengers." Among them was the author of this journal, Lucy Kendall, accompanied by her mother, a teenage sister, Annie, and Harry East, an old family friend who had helped the Kendalls bear family financial burdens.

Lucy, born and educated in England, was an articulate twenty-four-year-old. No longer an adolescent like Annie, she was sensitive to her surroundings and, above all, highly intelligent. Lucy recorded both the ship's daily routine as well as the human details of her long voyage. Whether written at sea or by overlanders, such diaries became virtual live companions, onto whose pages their writers could pour out even intimate thoughts.

Although numerous women wrote overland diaries, there are few by those who traveled to California via Cape Horn.[1] Sometimes ship captains (particularly whalers who stayed at sea for years) brought along their wives, who kept records. But Lucy's account of a voyage that lasted 137 days, from May to October 1852, stands almost alone in its excellence.[2]

The twenty-thousand-mile trip to California via the Cape Horn route might take as much as two hundred days at sea. In March of 1849, the head of the family, Joseph Kendall, had boarded the three-masted bark *Canton* for San Francisco. That year alone 775 ships cleared eastern ports for California. Kendall's trip on the *Canton* took 188 days to complete. After a brief stay in the Sierra goldfields, he sent back enough money for his family's trip. His wife Charlotte paid $250 for each passage, or a total of $1000 for herself, her two daughters, and Harry East.

The voyage from coast to coast was a complicated one that involved crossing the tropics twice, over a period that might well last four to nine months—in both hot and cold weather. Bypassing Rio de Janeiro and Bahia, a "long easting" was necessary in order to clear Brazil's Cape St. Roque, the most easterly point of South America. This maneuver helped sailing vessels take advantage of strong northeastern trade winds.

While some clippers averaged over two hundred nautical miles per day, Lucy recorded that at times the *Josephine* was becalmed, seeming hardly to be moving. After Commodore Matthew Fontaine Maury, however, published his new *Wind and Current Charts* (1855), a number of beautiful clippers—among them the *Flying Cloud* as well as the *Swordfish* and *Andrew Jackson*—were able to round Cape Horn more rapidly. Light in weight, they did this by also cutting down the number of nautical miles formerly required.[3] In 1851, the year before Lucy's voyage, the 1,310-ton *Witchcraft,* with her figurehead displaying a grim Salem witch on a broomstick, set a new record: she sailed from New York to San Francisco in only ninety-seven days. In 1852 the *Flying Fish* set another record with a passage of ninety-two days. Most ships took much longer. Unlucky ones foundered in heavy gales, forced to drift off a given course until the weather improved. Furthermore, like the *Josephine,* not all sailing vessels were even seaworthy.

After 1848, when California's great Gold Rush began, some forty thousand persons reached that former Mexican province by sea or land. Those who chose the Cape Horn route were mostly young, some in their twenties. Passengers themselves hastily organized joint-stock companies for the voyage to California. Since the days of the hide-and-tallow trade, well before the Gold Rush era, eastern entrepreneurs (among them the Aspinwall, Howland, and Vanderbilt shipping firms) owned most of the vessels bound for San Francisco. However, William T. Coleman and other San Francisco merchants also operated vessels on both coasts of South America.

By 1852 more than one hundred clipper vessels sailed toward San Francisco from eastern ports. Ships of all sizes, from small yachts to vessels like the *Great Republic,* which weighed 4,555 tons, headed for the alluring goldfields of California. The *Josephine* and other vessels were hastily fitted to carry passengers. Some of these Cape Horn ships were barely seaworthy. They creaked and groaned, rolling about helplessly in heavy storms. A surprising number ultimately were sunk in heavy waters or lost at sea.

Seamen referred to the route below the South American mainland, first rounded in 1513 by Vasco Balboa, as travel via "old Cape Stiff." Some ships that made it through that maritime graveyard sailed on to China. Others would end their days rotting at anchor on the San Francisco waterfront, their crews having left for the Sierra gold streams.

The California gold rush had, indeed, greatly enhanced opportunities for fabulous profits in the Pacific Coast trade. The scarcity of food and supplies led to extortionate prices for goods of all sorts. This hastened the need for rapid shipping of merchandise to San Francisco—from boots and shoes to shovels and hammers. When speed, however, was not a requisite, the Cape Horn route was more economical than transshipment across the Isthmus of Panama. The latter route, however, usually took only several months, as opposed to an average of six months around the Horn. Until the building of a transcontinental railroad line across the

United States in 1869, the Cape Horn route remained the best way to ship heavy mining machinery and other bulk cargoes to the west coast; it was, however, too slow for the transportation of mail from the east.

Lucy Kendall's trip coincided with the golden age of American sailing vessels, with the peak of the clipper era occurring during the years 1850–55. Alongside those magnificent ships, many less famous vessels lumbered toward the west coast of North America. The *Josephine*, commanded by Captain William Jameson, carried two heavy cannons aboard and was primarily a carrier of bulk merchandise. She was, furthermore, a leaky vessel. Whenever warm weather expanded her seams, she required pumping out, sometimes at the rate of three hundred gallons per hour.[4]

The voyage around the tip of South America, through the Straits of Magellan, came to be known as "the white-collar route." On passenger lists were teachers, ministers, merchants, and tradesmen. Although not the quickest way to California, it was the cheapest, costing only several hundred dollars, with food and freight charges included. Also, it was the route preferred by women, for one could make the entire trip without disembarking in Central America and crossing the jungle areas of the Isthmus of Panama.[5]

But the long Cape Horn voyage was a boring one. Passengers made the best of seemingly endless days aboard with banjo, fiddle, and games, including wagering on the ship's arrival date. Walks on deck and the playing of chess were high points of each day—in addition to most welcome hot meals. Lucy was a minor artist as well as, like her mother, an accomplished pianist. They had brought along music books and a small upright piano, which was stored below decks. In her cabin Lucy passed the time by drawing and reading. In addition to the Bible, among the volumes she treasured were Harriet Beecher Stowe's new book, *Uncle Tom's Cabin,* as well as Sir Walter Scott's *Ivanhoe*. Her father, aboard the *Canton,* was an even more avid Bible reader.

While at sea, sewing was yet another important daily activity for the women, while the men played cards, dominoes, and backgammon. Bathing (and for the men shaving), as well as putting on clean clothes at tea time, took on special importance—as did shaking out bedbugs from one's linen and airing out smelly hair mattresses on deck. At night, when the skies were clear, one could stargaze at such unfamiliar constellations as the Southern Cross.

And there was the daily journal, which Lucy sometimes wrote on deck while sitting on a coil of rope. Lucy recorded that, on occasion, tensions ran high. Once, after the inebriated cook burned the soup, the captain tied him to the ship's rigging and flogged him severely—despite the fact that flogging was forbidden by American law, partly as a result of the strenuous efforts of Richard Henry Dana, author of *Two Years Before the Mast* (1841), to reform legislation covering seamen's rights. The *Josephine*'s cook saved the bloody rope with which he was beaten after his ordeal, but whether he ever brought charges against Captain Jameson is uncertain.

Although only the crew of the *Josephine* was actually forced to witness the brutal beating, the effect on young Lucy was traumatic. In her own words, she fell into a state of "gloom and depression." Mixed with nostalgia for the home she had left, Lucy's feelings about the megalomaniac captain remained ambivalent. She considered him to be a martinet who was hard as nails and whose only redeeming feature was dispensing hot tea and a hard biscuit to his crew each night and morning. Lucy experienced varying moods of sadness and elation exacerbated by lack of exercise, which softened up all such voyagers. Seasickness too was a common affliction. The unappealing antidote to such queasiness, according to Richard Henry Dana, was to be found by "swallowing cold salt beef and bisquit."

Passengers on the long Cape Horn route sought any means available to escape boredom. Each vessel celebrated holidays in different ways. Aboard the *Rising Sun,* the Fourth of July was marked by blowing bugles, playing martial music, a deckside reading of the Declaration of Independence, speech-making, and a dinner of roast goose, plum pudding, mince pie, figs, and nuts. These delicacies were a welcome respite from fried ham with hard and soft tack. The *Josephine* carried fifteen dozen live chickens, some turkeys (a few of the poultry escaped into the briny deep), as well as sheep, pigs, and a passenger's two pet canaries. In addition, a Newfoundland dog named "Rover" was also aboard.[6]

Lucy's diary reveals that she did not think highly of the revelry that accompanied crossing the equator. On some ships, including her father's, the mythological Neptune was hauled up out of the ocean by dowsing the uninitiated with pails of seawater. Both her diary and that of her father record disapproval of the heavy drinking that accompanied these renowned festivities. Because of the heat, revelers on the *Canton* ended up sleeping on deck. This could prove dangerous: should heavy weather appear during the night, a ship could pitch forward or roll from side to side.

As the *Josephine* hugged the south Atlantic coastline of today's Argentina, its passengers crowded the rails to view flying fish. In certain locations other varieties also were in abundance. In good weather, bonito, albacore, mackerel, and schools of porpoises played round the ship's bow. Lucy's father, while traveling on the *Canton,* had seen electric eels, which he described as "all on fire."[7] Sometimes pilot fish, tiny creatures who swam near bigger fish for sustenance and protection, accompanied sharks.

An occasional albatross or pelican, floating in the wake of the *Josephine,* was shot or hooked aboard merely to measure its wide wingspread. On another vessel, the *North Bend,* passengers were able to entice more than a hundred cape pigeons to follow the ship by throwing pieces of bread over the stern; on the *Josephine,* they were captured with fishhooks baited with pork. The crew also tried to catch bonitos and sardines in order to supplement the boring daily ship fare. A staple was salt pork; when combined with potatoes, the greasy dish was called souse. Fried ham, biscuits, and coffee comprised the usual breakfast.[8]

Food and drink were important matters. At one point Lucy complained that "our water is beginning to taste very bad." An oily pipe had polluted the vessel's water tank. On most ships, sediment frequently covered the bottom of one's cup so that drinks came to smell as bad as bilgewater. As a result, cholera became a potentially fatal danger. During squalls, therefore, ship crews regularly sought to capture fresh rainwater. On the *Canton,* Lucy's father drank an alternative mixture of molasses and vinegar. This beverage was called switchel—to which brandy was sometimes added.

In his *Two Years Before the Mast,* Richard Henry Dana had described the annual northern migration of whales along the Pacific coast. The *Josephine* also encountered numbers of these huge sea mammals. Indeed, it was necessary to keep a sharp eye out for iron-grey-colored humpbacks that might at any time break out of the water, crossing in front of the ship's bow. Lucy and her fellow passengers also spotted massive finbacks and bowheads that quietly passed by only a few yards away from the ship. Others might suddenly emerge from below the surface with their great tail fins thrust high above the water line. Pursued by whaling vessels for their blubber and sperm oil, these behemoths were potentially dangerous creatures.

Unknown to the passengers, there was a far more risky peril aboard the ship itself, for the *Josephine* had taken on a cargo of volatile explosives (1,500 kegs of gunpowder) as well as coal and turpentine. These items, as well as the camphor and alcohol vials also aboard, were all in short supply in post–Gold Rush California. Had Lucy and her mother known what the ship carried below her decks, they would have embarked on another vessel. After they learned about the ship's lethal cargo, they came to fear the worst, especially during each lightning-filled thunderstorm.

As their ship proceeded past the Falkland Islands, they encountered other vessels. It was not uncommon for several ships to be in company at sea. Lucy writes that the captain, using a megaphone, "was able to 'speak a Spanish brig.'" It "came quite near and was crowded with . . . a mean-looking set of soldiers. . . . Our flag was raised and drawn up and down, according to the formalities of seamen and answered the same way. Longitude and latitude were exchanged, and after much waving of hats the courtesies were over and each ship proceeded on its way."

Several days later an English vessel lay alongside in order "to buy sea biscuits and rice." In exchange, its captain promised to take some passenger letters to Liverpool. During that very day Lucy saw nine vessels on the horizon, which lessened her feeling of being alone on the high seas. In the trough of heavy seas, other ships were sometimes out of sight until they came nearby. When the ocean was not too rough, passengers and crew members would actually board other ships, exchanging information about their respective voyages.[9] Occasionally she also saw bottles floating alongside the ship. It was not unusual for these to be retrieved and refloated with messages added.

By August 1, 1852, the first part of the *Josephine*'s voyage had almost been completed. She was now well beyond Buenos Aires. But the most frightening part of the journey lay ahead—either the rounding of Cape Horn or passage through the Straits of Magellan. Some vessels took four to six weeks getting through the straits. Diarists described them as very narrow, resembling Norwegian fjords, with the hulks of vessels that had foundered strewn about the rocky banks.

The *Josephine* had already weathered heavy gales and ever-changing winds near the Atlantic tip of South America. Now fierce waves washed over the deck, which sometimes was covered by snow and hail. Everyone who made this trip complained of the heavy weather. Aboard the *Canton*, Lucy's father was knocked out of his berth while crockery and food "flew in every direction" (see his *A Landsman's Voyage to California,* p. 100).

On the *Josephine,* seagulls wafting in the wind above were but one signal that she was approaching the straits. With his ship tossing about aimlessly, Captain Jameson decided that entering the narrow and windy straits would be too dangerous. This was a wise move—although Sir Francis Drake, followed by many other mariners, had successfully navigated the treacherous Straits of Magellan as early as 1578. Much later, new Lateen sails never quite corrected a ship's tendency to drift leeward onto the rocks that lined that passageway. Hence it was that Captain Jameson elected to "double the Cape," westward, which was itself a rough, chilling, eight-day experience.

As if rounding the rocky shoals of Cape Horn in mountainous seas were not dangerous enough, a sailor, with a lighted candle in hand, wandered below decks where the ship's gunpowder was stored. On most ships fires were forbidden, except in the cook's galley. The captain, furious about this foolhardiness, considered flogging the offending crew member.

6

Lucy and her fellow passengers would experience yet another traumatic event. An unfortunate sailor was suddenly washed overboard when the sea swelled up over the ship's railing. The *Josephine*'s passengers were horrified that Captain Jameson did nothing to save the seaman—the ocean tides were apparently much too turbulent to lower a skiff. Furthermore, there was no memorial service held aboard the *Josephine,* while other ships sometimes held elaborate rituals whenever someone died.[10]

After entering the Pacific leg of the voyage, all aboard were relieved to learn that the captain intended to stop at Valparaiso, Chile. Some ships put in at the Galapagos Islands for wood and water; Juan Fernandez Island was also a favorite landing spot. Lucy's father recorded that the *Canton* took on sixty turtles at nearby Chatham and other islands.[11] It was also not unusual for vessels to put in at Callao on the Peruvian mainland, further up the west coast. But the *Josephine*'s only stop before San Francisco was at Valparaiso.

Lucy's description of the latter city and its inhabitants is a full and valuable one. With the ship's flour turning wormy and even its bad water supply running low, and with only a dozen chickens and a few turkeys left, all hands were relieved to taste fresh food and drink again. After they landed, the tiresome shipboard diet was temporarily left behind for a few days as the passengers gorged themselves on bananas and unfamiliar mangoes, papayas, and other exotic fruit. In addition to relishing cake and chocolate in a local French restaurant, there were colorful cotton dresses (as well as cloth, which was far more expensive in California) to be bought. Bullfights, cockfights, donkey rides, and village *fandango* celebrations never failed to astound Yankee visitors to Latin America.

Lucy's mother was relieved to find a letter from her husband at Valparaiso's post office, written from San Francisco. She and her daughters also were invited aboard the United States man-of-war *Rariton*. But after too brief a visit—accompanied by toasts with sherry and champagne—they again set sail on the final leg of their trip to California. Not only did the weather improve after the *Josephine* re-crossed the equator, but an intriguing new passenger had joined the ship's company at Valparaiso. He was a charming political exile who turned out to be an aide to his fellow countryman, the Hungarian revolutionary hero Louis Kossuth. Traveling incognito under the name of Maurice Weisberger, Kossuth's aide told the impressionable Lucy all about his supposedly exciting covert life in Europe.[12]

Off the west coast of Mexico, they encountered one of the fastest of all clipper ships, the cleancut *Witch of the Wave* out of Boston. She weighed 1,498 tons and sometimes carried close to 2,000 more in cargo. Despite such heavy loads, the *Witch* repeatedly won annual races from the east coast of North America to San Francisco, Hawaii, and China. She had hailed the *Josephine* only because its master, Captain Benjamin Tay (misspelled "Jay" in Lucy's diary), wished to purchase some potatoes. The haughty captain, featured in the *Illustrated London News,* wore kid gloves and gave no orders to anyone but the officer of the watch.

Finally there came that welcome day when the *Josephine* sighted the California coast. After encountering a turbulent stretch of water between the rocky Farallon Islands and the Golden Gate, they at last limped into a great, capacious bay. There Lucy saw dozens of other ships from all over the world anchored on the San Francisco waterfront. This bustling new metropolis, no longer called Yerba Buena, would become the center of her future life. Lucy's diary stops abruptly on October 20, 1852, upon her arrival.[13]

She had written an exceptional account, which now joins the company of other diaries that have found their way into print. The romantic era of graceful sailing vessels was about to give way to the age of steam and maritime mechanization. This makes Lucy Kendall's journal all the more valuable. About sailing-ship diaries written during trips around the Horn, John Pomfret has written: "As new materials are discovered, and published, the historical importance of this great migration by sea in the occupation and settlement of California will be[come more] firmly established."[14]

The story of Lucy Kendall's subsequent life in California, and of her marriage to William Francis Herrick, a talented artist, is also recounted in this book. Herrick arrived in 1853, after a 106-day voyage aboard the famed vessel *Westward Ho*.[15] The couple encountered, and were soon preoccupied with, stirring vigilante activities that would shake San Francisco society for months on end.

Their family eventually consisted of seven daughters and two sons. Lucy lived until June 11, 1906. Her husband died in the same year. Both are buried at Mountain View Cemetery in Oakland.[16]

NOTES

1. Two diaries by women who rounded Cape Horn in 1852 are in the Huntington Library. These are by Alphia Follansbee (HM37545) and Charlotte Gardner (HM39179). Gardner's husband was captain of the ship *Sarah Parker*. Follansbee also traveled with her husband aboard the *Greenfield*. But their accounts are prosaic, mostly concerned with details about weather and daily routine aboard ship. Other journals by women are analyzed in Joan Druett, ed., *She Was a Sister Sailor* (Mystic, Conn.: Mystic Seaport Museum, 1992) and in Druett, *Petticoat Whalers: Whaling Wives at Sea,* 1820–1920 (Auckland, New Zealand: Collins, 1991). See also Anne Mackay, ed., *She Went A-Whaling* (Orient, N.Y.: Oysterponds Historical Society 1995). A highly literate Atlantic diary is transcribed in Catherine Petroski, *A Bride's Passage: Susan Hathorn's Year Under Sail* (Boston: Northeastern University Press, 1996).

2. Lucy seems to have counted only days at sea, not port stops. Carl C. Cutler's *Greyhounds of the Sea: The Story of the American Clipper Ship.* (New York: G. P. Putnam's Sons, 1930) states that the voyage took 147 days. Her father's journey to Yerba Buena (San Francisco) is told in *A Landsman's Voyage to California. . . . An Account of the Voyage 'Round the Horn of the Bark* Canton (San Francisco: Taylor and Taylor, 1935). Joseph had joined a group of sixty persons banded together as the Island City Mining and Trading Association. Two vessels named *Canton* were built— one in 1840 at Wiscasset, Maine, the other the next year at Cranberry Isles, Maine. See Forrest R. Holdcamper, comp., *List of American-flag Merchant Vessels that Received Certificates of Enrollment or Registry at the Port of New York, 1789–1867* (Washington, D.C.: U.S. National Archives and Records Service, General Services Administration, 1968).

3. The literature about America's clipper ship era is voluminous. Raymond A. Rydell's *Cape Horn to the Pacific* (Berkeley: University of California, 1952) is indispensable.

4. *The Portsmouth* (N.H.) *Journal* for February 28, 1852, announced the launching of the 170-foot *Josephine*. Its owner was General Joseph Andrews of Salem, Massachusetts. She was built of white oak and described as "truly handsome" with a central cabin forty-five feet in length. See Ray Brighton, *Clippers of the Port of Portsmouth and the Men Who Built Them* (Portsmouth, N.H.: Portsmouth Marine Society, 1985). Also, for other details on the *Josephine,* see William Armstrong Fairburn, *Merchant Sail,* ed. Ethel M. Ritchie (Center Lovell, Maine: Fairburn Marine Educational Foundation, n.d.), vol. 5, pp. 3067, 3092. Two previous *Josephines* were actually launched; the first had come off the ways in 1840 at Richmond, Virginia. The second was built in 1844 in Rochester, Massachusetts where the famous *Flying Cloud* had been launched (see Holdcamper, passim).

5. The authority on the Central American approach to California, John Haskell Kemble, in his *The Panama Route, 1848–1869* (Berkeley: University of California, 1943), p. 207, states that twenty-one members of California's third legislature had reached California via Cape Horn while forty-six came overland and thirty-five by way of Panama. See *New York Herald,* 22 December 1853; *Panama Star and Herald,* 14 May 1853.

6. Regarding ship cargoes, see Basil Lubbock, *The Down Easters: American Deep-Water Sailing Ships, 1869–1929* (Boston: C. E. Lauriat Co., 1919), passim.

7. *A Landsman's Voyage,* p. 87.

8. John E. Pomfret, ed., *California Gold Rush Voyages, 1848–1849: Three Original Narratives* (Westport, Conn.: Greenwood Press, 1954), p. 68.

9. The manuscript diary of Enoch Jacobs, a 29-year-old merchant aboard the ship *Edward Everett,* records (p. 13) such an exchange of personnel. His voyage from Boston to San Francisco took 167 days. See Huntington Library Manuscript 328.

10. For a vivid account of a shipboard death, see the manuscript diary of William H. Saxton (p. 74), who traveled to California on the *Brooklyn* in 1849. Saxton also describes a man washed overboard on that ship. Huntington Library Manuscript 17011, p. 28.

11. At the Cocos Islands the *Canton* took on twenty-seven casks of fresh water as well as mangoes. See *A Landsman's Voyage,* pp. 112–22.

12. Kossuth wished to create an independent Hungarian nation. In December of 1851 he had arrived in America as a political refugee fleeing from Austrian authorities. Weisberger was ostensibly en route to Minnesota where he hoped to found a Hungarian colony. Attracted to Lucy, he evidently returned to San Francisco in 1856, disappointed that she had, meanwhile, married.

13. In 1858 the *Josephine* was described as at Honolulu unloading guano from Jarvis Island, according to Octavius Howe and Frederick Matthews, *American Clipper Ships, 1833–1858,* vol. I (Salem, Mass.: Marine Research Society, 1926), p. 203. Soon thereafter, in June 1859, she was destroyed by fire at St. Louis Harbor in Mauritius (see memorandum from Irene Stachura, National Park Service, to Marcia A. Good).

14. Pomfret, p. ix.

15. The best summary of this and other California voyages is in Arthur H. Clark, *The Clipper Ship Era* (New York: G. P. Putnam's Sons, 1911), pp. 289ff. Less useful is Helen La Grange, *Clipper Ships of America and Great Britain, 1833–1869* (New York: G. P. Putnam's Sons, 1936) which, however, describes many ships en route to San Francisco.

16. Consult Amy R. Russell, "The Early Years of William Francis Herrick," in *California Historical Society Quarterly* 26, no. 3 (September 1947): 217–32.

SOUVENIR OF ENGLAND

MEMORIES OF CHILDHOOD YEARS by Lucy Kendall Herrick

These "Memories of Childhood Years" were gathered by Lucy Kendall Herrick in 1902 and 1906 for her daughter. Part was written "because it is Margaret's birthday"; part was a memorandum jotted down at her dictation; a small part was only spoken. A few facts and dates have been verified; otherwise this preface to her life stands almost as she herself gave it in those few years before her death on June 11, 1906.

Pencil sketch of Langford Farm, attributed to Joseph Kendall.

I was born in Bicester, Oxfordshire, England, on the 25th day of October in the year 1828, and shortly thereafter given the name of Lucy Fiennes Kendall. Lucy was the name of my mother's dearest friend, Lucy Williams, the sister of Edward Williams, the artist,[1] who painted several portraits of my mother's family, and the name Fiennes was that of Sir Twistleton Fiennes, of Lord Saye and Sele's family, a fox-hunting acquaintance of my father's. He was not a close friend, but on the morning I was born he met my father in the street in Bicester, so I have been told, and greeted him with, "Morning, Kendall, you are looking very smiling today! What has happened?"

"I have a right to smile, Sir T.," was the happy reply. "My wife has just presented me with a little daughter."

"Is that so?" said the other. "Well, give the baby my name, and I shall stand godfather, and here are five guineas[2] to buy her a rattle."

And so in the spring of 1829, at St. Edburg's Church, I was christened Lucy Fiennes Kendall; Sir Twistleton was entered in the record as my godfather, and that was the end of the matter!

My birthplace, twelve miles from the city of Oxford, was an unimportant town from which my father and mother, Joseph and Charlotte Kendall, removed when I was two years old.

Business had not been successful for my father; so he went to London with the hope of bettering his prospects, and left my mother and me (the baby) with my maternal grandparents, William and Anne Paxton, who lived at Langford Farm.

Some old friends, having met my father, told him they were about to sail for America the next day, and he became imbued with the determination to accompany them.

He at once communicated with my mother, and told her that if she wanted to go with him, she must come to London by the twelve o'clock stagecoach, there not being any railroads in that part of the country at that time (1830). My grandparents consented to her going, making the stipulation, however, that I should be left with them until my parents were settled in the new country.

It was then that the sister of my mother, who was like a twin to her, received me as her charge. It was under her sweet and tender care in that lovely home that I remained until I was nearly five years old. Aunt Mary's motherly love has followed me through a long and eventful life. She was about nineteen and her devotion was exceptional.

One night after putting me safely to bed, and while singing a little song, which was a particular favorite with me:

I'd be a butterfly, born in a bower,
Where roses and lilies and violets meet,
Culling the sweet from flower to flower . . .

she broke off and exclaimed, "Your mother has come!"

Now I had always been told that I *had* a mother in another land, and that she would come for me some day; but who can tell of the anguish that filled my heart as I heard that *that* mother had arrived to take me from my idolized grandparents and auntie.

I would not go down to see her; and yet after my aunt had gone to meet her sister, I stole quietly out of bed and peeped into the hallway. And even now I can see my mother with her rejoicing relatives around her as she called for her child!

By and by I crept down alone, to the dining-room door; and peeping in, I saw the stranger by the fire with my grandfather. In a moment I was seized and carried in to meet her for the first time after nearly three years. And this is my earliest memory of my mother.

It was the holiday season and the following day she unpacked her gifts for me. I became the possessor of many rare and precious things; among them a white fur muff and tippet, and a small music box in a tortoise-shell case—both from Paris. At night as I went to sleep, I was often allowed to have the music box under my pillow, to hear it play either a gay little French waltz, or the tune to Sir Walter Scott's "Lullaby to an Infant Chief."

But it took months for my mother to win me, for my auntie had won the affection of my earliest years. And I whispered to Aunt Mary that I did not want to go to America with the woman in the red shawl!

Langford was indeed a lovely home. My grandpa had great taste, and knowledge of agricultural and horticultural pursuits. The garden was a marvel of beauty, with hanging vines and rare flowers. The gravel walks were rolled and kept free of weeds, while the ivy that covered the house was trimmed about the windows each week, making it as some travelers styled it, the beau-ideal of an English farmhouse. The Paxton family did not own Langford, as it was part of an entailed estate belonging at that time to Sir Gregory Osborne Page Turner for whom my grandfather acted as steward or agent, but it was held on twenty-year leases; and the farm, the house, and the grounds were cared for as meticulously as if they had been my grandfather's own.

As a young man, Grandfather Paxton had first been employed on Sir Gregory's estate in Derbyshire, where his brothers remain[ed], but later he had been sent to take charge of the estate in Oxfordshire. There he lived at Langford in a comfortable home with beautiful gardens and four

Baby Lucy, pencil sketch by Edward Williams, ca. 1832–33.

*Lucy's grandfather,
William Paxton.*

gardeners to take care of them. Such rare flowers, abundant fruits, and choice vegetables as grew there! The brick walls of the kitchen garden were painted black to hold the sun, and the peaches and nectarines, trained flat upon them, ripened delicious fruit. There were rows of gooseberries and of currants, black, red, and white, and there was a grapehouse too, the vines being planted outside the walls and then coaxed through openings to the inner side and allowed to grow in profusion up to the glass roof.

In the garden, directly opposite the entrance door of the house, was placed the baptismal font of Edward the Confessor, an antique possession of Sir Gregory's and valued at two hundred pounds.

Sir Gregory was an expert on all ancient possessions. He owned seventy gold watches, and his drawing-room windows at Battlesden Park, which I have seen, cost a thousand pounds. Stained glass, cabinets of curios, and similar extravagances threatened to ruin him, and because of his eccentricities his relatives placed him in confinement for a time. He was very devoted to my grandfather, however, and once placed a purse of gold in his hands.

Langford had many charms, and people dwelling in the town of Bicester would walk down to survey the beauty of its well-kept lawns and flowers; a succession of the latter coming in with every season of the year, from the snowdrops and crocuses that first bloomed in the spring, to the Rose of Sharon, the laburnum, and Crown Imperial of the summer months. All this I can recall and the delight I had skipping about my grandfather while he looked for an errant weed that no gardener dared overlook on the grounds.

At the foot of the garden was the countinghouse where my grandpa kept his accounts in his exact and orderly way, and where he paid the farm laborers every week. On one day in particular, shortly after my mother had returned, the wages were placed in very precise piles of shillings and pence on the counter. I was told strictly not to touch. Perhaps this very order was more than a lively four-year-old could well endure, or perhaps I wished to show the strange woman from New York that this was one place where I might do as I wished. Be that as it may, on this occasion I swept all the money—with one whisk of my hand—to the four corners of the room. Whereupon my mother promptly spanked me (the first spanking I had ever received) and my grandpa stood by, wringing his hands and crying, "Charlotte, Charlotte, you are killing the child!"

I am afraid that I resented my mother's discipline at that time, as it seemed to me she had not the right to punish me. My Uncle George had taught me to call my stomach my breadbasket and Mamma thought the expression a vulgar one. She also disapproved of the song—

> A frog he would a-wooing go
> Heigh-ho said Rowley . . .

which she pronounced "immoral"; the line "whether his mother would let him or no" being calculated to teach disobedience in the young! She was pleased, however, that I had learned, also from Uncle George, to sing "Rule Britannia," perfectly correctly from beginning to end.

Beyond the grounds at Langford, two fields away, was the London Road, and through these fields was the entrance to the home and garden. Old elms were seen on the road, and now and then a few favorite sheep would browse beneath their shade, and I could dance a ring around them. And often when my grandpa would ride over the fields on his big horse, I would be allowed to ride behind him on a pillion, my arms scarcely able to reach around his very ample waist.

Once I did venture alone beyond these fields out on the London Road, and along the thoroughfare which was really dangerous, as cattle and horses were driven to the Bicester Market that way. I knew the shops in Bicester, and went along as fast as I could to the chief dry goods shop and demanded fifty yards of calico! I knew the head clerk, Sammy Burrows, and when he said, "But my little dear, you couldn't carry fifty yards," I left the store much incensed and returned home to find how much I had alarmed the mother and aunt for whom I had made the journey. They had been piecing patch-work for a quilt (which later followed me to America), and as they had been in want of more material, I had thought to procure some for them in Bicester.

Beyond the Langford grounds and well-tilled fields, beyond the London Road, and further on, rose a hill, on the summit of which was a wood—a wonder of tall trees and undergrowth and the resort of huntsmen from Oxford and the surrounding country seeking to drive the fox to shelter. It was a grand sight to see the red-coats (or "pinks" as they were called) with their splendid horses gathering on the hill with the hounds, waiting to start on their race. My uncles used to ride with them, and I thought they looked very handsome indeed in their bright coats, blue trousers, and boots so shiny I could almost see my reflection in their surface. But at Langford the hunt was carefully and anxiously watched for fear that the huntsmen might ride over the cornfields, the like of which could not be matched in the county. On several occasions they did ride, pell-mell, across our fields, and were later obliged to pay for the damage.

One of my favorite friends at Langford was the old shepherd who used to come into the basement kitchen for his noonday dinner. This kitchen with its flagstone floor and great, open fireplace where the food was cooked on the hearth, was a place I loved. There I could watch the kitchen-boy turning the meat on the spit, and often I was given a piece of bread on a long fork and told I might have a "dip in the pan"; then I would catch the juices in the dripping-pan with my piece of bread and this I relished exceedingly. As I sat in a corner to take my fill, the old man, who always wore a smock frock, as did the other laborers, would tell me stories over his dinner of bread and bacon, throwing bits to his shepherd dog as he talked.

Sundays were quiet, peaceful days with a Sabbath feeling in the very air. All the family went together into Bicester by wagonette, behind a fine pair of horses. Aunt Mary in her long, red cloak, bonnet, pantalettes, and mitts, carried a bead reticule which contained a pocket handkerchief, money for the collection, and a couple of peppermint lozenges for me should the sermon cause in me a desire to fidget. She was a very pretty auntie, with many beaux who usually wished to escort her home from church, and sometimes, I am afraid, I was a little in the way!

My grandmother, Anne Pitkin (maiden name), had been one of a family of lacemakers at Woburn, where my grandparents were married. I have in my possession some of the wooden bobbins, weighted with glass beads, and still wound with the fine thread with which she made English thread lace. Occasionally, when asked, she would get out a round basket which held the hard pillow on which she still kept a pattern of lace, half-finished but still held in place by its pins. The work was too fine for her eyes when I knew her, but she greatly enjoyed showing me how she threw the bobbins over each other, twisting the lace about the pins to make the pattern. I also have a piece of her wedding dress—a lawn, trimmed in this lace. Grandmother, with her small hands and feet, must have been a beauty in it.

My grandfather was one of eight children, and he had inherited the same love of flowers and gardening as did his youngest brother, my great-uncle Joseph. It was this very Uncle Joseph (architect, horticulturalist, and, for ten years before his death, member of Parliament for Coventry) who at the age of twenty-three (in 1826), and shortly before I was born, was given charge of the Duke of Devonshire's estate, Chatsworth. And in 1851 he was knighted by Queen Victoria for designing the Crystal Palace, which was a sort of glorified evolution of the glass houses at Chatsworth.

16

When Joseph, the baby of the family, was a very young child, his father died and his mother, who was poor, sent him to be brought up in the home of his eldest brother, William (my grandfather), where he lived until he was twelve years old. He was about the age of my mother and older uncles and grew up as one of them. However, he became determined to earn his own living and at an early age sought employment, first at Battlesden, then later in Chiswick Gardens, managed by the Horticultural Society. There he was put in charge of creepers and new plants. One day in passing, the Duke of Devonshire, whose estate adjoined these grounds, surprised him reading, and inquired what book he had by him. "Latin, sir," Joseph Paxton replied; and the Duke was so pleased with his intelligence and handsome appearance that he took him under his care and had him educated as an architect and horticulturist. He was even taken abroad, where he rode in the nobleman's carriage. There on the continent, my great-uncle made the plans of eighty cottages, which were afterwards built in the village of Edensor for the use of the gardeners employed on the Duke's estate at Chatsworth.

When given charge by the Duke, Joseph Paxton directed one hundred gardeners; his knowledge and scientific acquirements led him to write many volumes of botany, nine of which he presented to Queen Victoria when she made a royal visit to Chatsworth. He caused an artificial mountain to be raised on the estate. Foreign countries were sent to for botanical specimens; the water-lily called "Victoria Regia" was brought to England and flowered by him in the Great Stove, or hothouse.

In 1850 he designed the Crystal Palace for the Great Exhibition of 1851. Some men were in a train, discussing how the building should be raised, when one of them said, "Here is Joseph Paxton; hear what he says." My great-uncle then and there made the preliminary design for a building of glass and iron—a great innovation at the time.

So did he go on. He married Sarah Bown, a sweet lady by whom he had a large family of children. He had a beautiful and costly mansion for himself on the Duke's grounds where many of the titled people of England came to visit him and to see the ducal estate. His income must have been immense.

In my grandfather's own family there were nine siblings, eight of whom were living when I was born—and all of them under my grandfather's roof. Such an affectionate family they were, and such good times as they had together. No wonder I thought of Langford as my own, true home!

I still can see us all about the table in the sitting-room in the evening: Grandfather, square, steel-rimmed spectacles on his nose, always with a candlestand at either shoulder, reading aloud from his newspapers or perhaps from Hannah More's works; Grandmother and my aunts at some knitting; and Uncle Jonas, who was only ten years older than I, teaching me how to make a cat's cradle with string. Sometimes to tease my grandfather, I would creep up behind him to blow out his candles and escape while he was groping in the dark. This then was the beloved home to which my mother returned just before New Year's, 1832, and the home from which she meant to take me.

After many years, memory comes to me of the time when a carriage was brought to the door, in which my mother and I were driven away by my Uncle Thomas, to London, to go on board the ship that was to take us to the father I did not know.

Aunt Mary was left behind, and the beloved grandparents, and the uncles who bore with me and petted me, and the sweet, young Aunt Liddy . . . all were left behind! Alas, how a child can suffer!

We sailed away in a brig, and after many perilous conditions in which mutiny was threatened, one day we landed; a gentleman with a kindly face clasped me to his arms, and thus I first remember my dear father.

NOTES

1. Edward Williams, landscape painter and son of Edward Williams, an engraver, was born in Lambeth in 1782. He studied under his uncle, James Ward, and was afterwards apprenticed to a carver and gilder. Trying his hand, however, at some moonlight landscapes, he was so successful that he took up painting again in earnest, and in 1814 and 1815 he exhibited at the Royal Academy. Later in life he painted much of the scenery of the Thames. He died at Barnes on the 24th day of June, 1855, leaving six sons, all of whom became artists. Three of them changed their names to Boddington, Percy, and Gilbert, respectively, in order to avoid confusion. Gilbert survived them all.

2. This was a handsome gift, indeed! A guinea was an English gold coin, last minted in 1813, equal to 21 shillings (1 pound = 20 shillings).

TO AND FROM AMERICA

1833–1849

View of Ventnor, Isle of Wight, at about the time the Kendalls lived there (1840–45).

Lucy Kendall Herrick wrote no more "Memorandums" of her childhood, but her gift for narrative was a vital one that kept many stories alive in her children's and grandchildren's memories. Bicester in Oxfordshire, where she was born, was a small market town, with St. Edburg's Church crowning a rise at the foot of the village. Nearly all of Bicester's twenty-two hundred inhabitants—including Lucy's father's family, the Kendalls, and her mother's family, the Paxtons—attended this church. When Charlotte Kendall returned from New York to Bicester for her child that Yuletide of 1832, her family was distressed to learn that on her stormy winter's voyage of six weeks across the North Atlantic, she had met a Baptist clergyman, the Reverend Octavius Onslow Winslow, who had converted her to that dissenting faith. Charlotte's conversion was sincere, but her convictions were tolerant. When she failed to convert her relatives too, an arrangement was made that Lucy should attend either church with no disagreement from anyone.

It was deemed wise that Charlotte Kendall should make a long visit in Bicester so that the child might become accustomed to her mother before they both sailed for New York to join Joseph Kendall. Those were days when migrating English men and women found separation more final, and communication more difficult than now. So the sad and overwhelming day of departure from England was postponed as long as possible for Lucy's sake. When, the following September, the time actually arrived, the Paxtons tried to make the occasion as happy a one as possible. Mrs. Kendall and Lucy were laden with gifts, and everyone wrote "undying sentiments" in Charlotte's new "Friendship Album."

Though the verses in it were written as early as March, it was not until the fall that the weeping Lucy was borne from Aunt Mary's arms and went off to London with her mother. There the Rev. Winslow was on the dock to bid them godspeed.

Having spent her fifth birthday on the high seas, and after "many vicissitudes," Lucy arrived in New York in early November, 1833. There she was met "on the Quay" by her "dear father" who took his wife and daughter to the little home at 65 Eldredge Street[1] on the Lower East Side, then "quite the genteel part of town."

Joseph Kendall was in the business of retailing paints, oils, and varnishes at 308 Grand Street, a short walk's distance from their home. This business was a congenial one, as he himself was an artist by temperament if not by occupation, and he loved to draw and paint in an amateur's way. In contrast to his wife, who had always been surrounded by the affection of dozens of relatives, Kendall seems to have been rather a lonely man, as he had been a lonely child. His mother had died at his birth in 1803, and his father died in Joseph's early childhood, leaving the boy to be brought up, not very happily, by a great-uncle. After he married Charlotte, Joseph Kendall, now that he had a wife to support, needed to seek a living further afield than Oxfordshire. Surely in America he could prove to his wife's relatives that he had the makings of a successful businessman. Unfortunately, as the years went on, he seems to have proven more thoroughly that in his business ventures, as in his migrations, he was inclined to be overly optimistic.

But in 1833 in New York, he welcomed his returning family with rejoicing, for he was always a most devoted husband and father.

It was a strange new life for the small Lucy in the bustling, growing, foreign city of thirty thousand inhabitants—very different from the peaceful quiet of Langford and the green, wet, level fields of Oxfordshire where she had spent her early years. Sometimes she and Mamma would walk down to South Street to the crowded docks, where they could see the ship sail away with letters to dear Grandpa or Aunt Mary. Or sometimes they would walk up East Broadway where the omnibuses, wagons, and carts rattled over the cobbles.

"Soon after our arrival in New York," she used to say, "New Year's Day was at hand and my mother allowed me to hang up a stocking for Santa Claus. I did; it was my father's . . . good and long. The contents I can remember; first an orange, then raisins, and then among other treasures, a book! Oh, the joy of it! *Holiday Tales!* In those days books were treasures indeed; even a small one was considered a prize and carefully cherished by its possessor. Another gift from my father was a pair of birds on a wire branch, which quivered delightfully when touched."

And early in 1834 she "began to learn," her first lesson being taught her at home by her mother. She was also sent to Sunday School at the Baptist Church not very far away in Oliver Street, and there "My first silk dress was an event! . . . On Sundays, when I put it on to go to Sunday School, I was given a pocket handkerchief and told that I was to 'dust the seat' before I sat down!"

New York was a much more worldly place than a quiet English market town such as Bicester, and Charlotte Kendall, devout Baptist though she was, nevertheless enjoyed the small elegancies of life. She liked to pay calls, and to know the latest styles, and being an expert needlewoman, made many charming things for herself and her small daughter.

On September 1, 1836, a long-wished-for second daughter was born to the Kendalls and named Mary Ann for the beloved aunt, recently married in England to Henry Flint. But to call a child by a name as formidable as Mary Ann would never do in a family devoted to diminutives, and Lucy's younger sister was "Annie" for the rest of her life.

Two years after the birth of his second daughter, Joseph Kendall received an offer for his business that seemed foolish to refuse, especially as his wife longed to return again to her English home and relatives. So in 1839 the Kendalls packed their belongings, said good-bye to the many friends they had made, and sailed away once more across the Atlantic, to land at Portsmouth. They took a stagecoach up through the leafy-green lanes and high roads of Hampshire and Berkshire to Newbury, where Aunt Mary now lived.[2]

"Early starts before daybreak were the rule, but nobody minded, for there was the music of the rattling harness and the ring of the horses' feet on the hard road, and the cheery toot of the guard's horn to warn some lazy pikeman, or hostler at the next change" of horses. Lucy may well have pointed out to the small Annie the early-morning life of the country-side: ". . . a market-cart or two, men in their smock frocks going to work, pipe in mouth, and the sun coming up to make the mist shine like silver gauze. . . . Sometimes they passed the hounds jogging along the road to a distant meet at the heels of the hackman's hack. . . . Or perhaps they met an early up-coach, and the coachmen would gather up their horses, and pass one another with the accustomed lift of the elbow, each team doing eleven miles an hour, and the passengers bouncing around inside."

Thomas Hughes, who wrote this description of English coaching in *Tom Brown's School Days,*[3] lived in Berkshire, not far from Newbury. And soon after the Kendalls arrived, they were introduced to Hughes by their relatives. The Kendalls also met young Harry East, "the boy but not the character" of the book. They did not know then that "Mr. Harry" would, a few years later, become a member of their own family by affectionate adoption.

The Newbury visit was a very happy one. Charlotte Kendall spent hours chatting of life in America, the family, and other cheerful matters, and the sisters sewed and read aloud to each other. In a few weeks their journey was resumed and the Kendalls went on, past the grey towers of Oxford into Bicester, where all the Paxtons, "the dear relatives" at Langford, were waiting to see them.

Anne Paxton was delighted to have them again, for her husband was more and more involved in estate matters and was often from home. There was plenty of room at Langford and the Kendalls, who had thought only to spend several months, found their visit lengthening into more than a year. Once more Lucy followed Grandma around with her egg basket, made doll's clothes with Aunt Liddy, rode about the lanes on her pony with Mamma, or played with the small Annie under the great trees in the garden. Sometimes they fed the pigeons who lived in the pigeon-cote in the barnyard or hunted for new kittens behind the cart-shed. That summer Aunt Liddy gave Lucy her first music lessons on Aunt Mary's old spinet. When Aunt Mary came to visit them, she played the spinet, Aunt Liddy sang in her lovely soprano voice, and Charlotte Kendall played the accordion or the flageolet, for the Paxtons were a very musical family. Thus Lucy learned many of the English songs and ballads that she loved all her life.

There were many visitors who came to Langford that summer of 1839 to see the returned travelers from America. Edward Williams came, and stayed to paint Charlotte Kendall's portrait, with its background of the Oxfordshire fields. Aunt Liddy whispered to Lucy that the artist had once been in love with her mother, in the days before Joseph Kendall had appeared. Lucy thought this very romantic.

She heard much talk at Langford of her Great-Uncle Joseph's incredible good fortune—the Grand Tour through Europe to the Levant with the Duke of Devonshire, a very great nobleman and one of the first gentlemen of England. Lucy heard, too, of the "Great Stove," or hothouse, then in the process of construction at Chatsworth. It was to be two hundred and seventy-seven feet long, with a central avenue wide enough for a horse and carriage to drive upon, and would be one of the wonders of the horticultural world. William Paxton, at Langford, was enormously proud of this younger brother, and told his family that he was not at all surprised to hear that Joseph had been offered the charge of the gardens at Windsor Castle at a salary of one thousand pounds a year. However, he stayed with the Duke, and later, as Lucy points out in her "Souvenir of England" (page 16), Joseph Paxton would be knighted by Queen Victoria for his creation of the Crystal Palace at the Great Exhibition of 1851.

Meanwhile, in the fall of 1840, an opportunity presented itself for Joseph Kendall to go into business in Ventnor on the Isle of Wight. This was not so far away and there might be semiannual visits to the dear relatives at Langford. Once more the Kendalls packed their belongings and drove away, down to Portsmouth and across the Solent to Ryde, over the downs of the Island, and on to the very tip of Britain, where the blue Atlantic stretches away to Spain.

Only twenty years before the Kendalls' arrival, Ventnor had been a mere hamlet whose few-score inhabitants had been engaged in crab and lobster fishing to supply the London markets. But about 1820 it had been discovered by Sir James Clark, a physician, whose published eulogy of its "salubrious climate" gave it an impetus to an amazing prosperity. Visitors to Ventnor found it a lovely spot. Even Joseph Paxton, who visited Ventnor during the Kendalls' residence, said (perhaps a trifle grandly), "I have visited nearly every place of note, from Stockholm to Constantinople, and have never seen anything more beautiful than this."

The Kendalls took a small place, "Poplar Cottage," where the tall trees grew in the garden and gave it the name, and two enormous whalebones in an arch quaintly formed the entrance gate. Charlotte Kendall, who had found Bicester rather quiet after New York, was delighted with Ventnor. It was in the country, yet was a fashionable place with plenty of life and activity going on. She and the children set about exploring the beauties of their new surroundings, which in the mild winter months were full of charm.

The Kendalls had not been in Ventnor long when Lucy and Annie were placed in Miss Warren's School for Young Ladies: Annie in the Infant School and Lucy, a little later, as a boarder. Here they remained for

Pencil drawing by Lucy while in school on the Isle of Wight, ca. 1844.

the next four years. But the summer of 1845 found hard times prevailing throughout England—"the hungry forties" as those years have been called—and Joseph Kendall's business began to suffer. It was decided that Lucy, now age sixteen, should leave school with the idea of returning only for French and piano lessons, but that Annie should continue at Miss Warren's as she was doing extremely well.

However, this state of affairs did not continue for long. Once again Joseph Kendall found opportunity presenting itself in America, and once more the Kendalls packed their belongings for a transatlantic voyage. Lucy was used to family upheavals by this time, and besides, she enjoyed a good long visit to Langford before the Kendalls sailed on what was to be Lucy's second voyage to New York.

The rapidly growing New York to which the Kendalls returned in 1845 was a city of sixty thousand inhabitants, then, as now, the largest city in the country. Those were the days when Polk was President and the American Merchant Marine had forced the British off the Western Ocean (as sailors called the North Atlantic at that time). The Kendalls returned to America by sailing ship as steamboats were only beginning to be used and were still considered highly dangerous.

The family took a house again, this time at 24 Market Street, at the corner of Henry where the Henry Street Settlement now stands. This home was a simple two-story wooden house with dormers in the attic. It was built flush with the sidewalk, like the other city houses around it, and in the rear was a small garden where Joseph Kendall, in his leisure moments, could grow flowers or even a few vegetables. Altogether it was a comfortable little place that Lucy was to call home for the next seven years.

Joseph Kendall again opened a paint shop, and seems to have been largely employed in what might now be termed "interior decorating," work such as marbling and gilding; sign-painting and "designing" occupied a large part of the business. At one time he directed forty men in the decorating of the Hudson River Steamboats, an exacting task, for the gorgeous interiors of these boats required most meticulous work and innumerable coats of paint in the elaborate decoration, which Joseph Kendall planned himself.

In the following summer of 1846, the Kendall family was increased by the arrival from Newbury of Harry East. He brought gifts and many messages from England. "Mr. Harry" had expected to stay with the Kendalls for only a few months while he observed life in the United States, but the months lengthened into years and he remained a beloved member of the Kendall family in America as long as he lived. The following summer the family was further increased by the arrival from England of Mrs. Kendall's niece and nephew, the son and daughter of her brother, Thomas Paxton. Charlotte Paxton, niece and namesake of Mrs. Kendall, came to live with them in Market Street. Thomas Paxton III boarded elsewhere. There was, after all, a limit to the capacity of the small house, which now sheltered six people besides Winnie, the kindly old Irish maid-of-all-work.

In the fall Lucy heard that her old drawing teacher at Miss Warren's School in Ventnor, Mrs. Miller, and her crotchety husband had come to America and were going to Boston to start a girl's school of their own. The Millers soon called on the Kendalls, and during the call asked Lucy if she would like to join them to teach the younger children music and French. The salary seemed an inducement to Lucy, who was now age eighteen and anxious to contribute to the family income. However, her experience in Boston proved to be an unhappy one. The food the Millers provided was not only poor but actually insufficient. As winter came on Lucy grew thinner and thinner, and she almost froze to death in her unheated attic room. When it seemed impossible to get warm or nourished, she bought crackers to supplement the frugal meals and Jamaica ginger to stir her circulation and warm herself a little.

When she went home to New York at Christmastime, her family was horrified at her appearance. "You shall never go back," Mrs. Kendall declared. But Lucy's efforts to recover her health seemed useless; the weeks passed and she seemed paler than ever. Mrs. Kendall had written in distress to her parents in England, and by the end of February a letter came from William Paxton insisting that Lucy return to Langford for a six-month visit. The sea voyage was sure to benefit her and she would have plenty of petting and care from her alarmed relatives. And Grandpa Paxton enclosed the funds for the voyage.

So, by the first of March, 1848, Lucy had set sail on the packet ship *Southampton*[4] under the care of Captain Morgan, a family friend. It was her fourth crossing of the Atlantic Ocean.

Mr. Harry's mother, Mrs. East of Newbury, came up to London to meet her after the voyage and put her on the train that now ran to Oxford. Country life at Bicester and lots of horse-riding gave Lucy's spirits and health a lift. Meanwhile, Charlotte's letters to her daughter, such as the cross-written one reproduced here, show that she was very much missed in New York. By the end of the summer her mother expected her to return home, but Lucy was having far too happy a time to think of going back yet, and Mrs. Kendall could not bring herself to insist that she return. The fall passed and winter came, and still Lucy did not return. She might even marry and stay in England, she wrote.

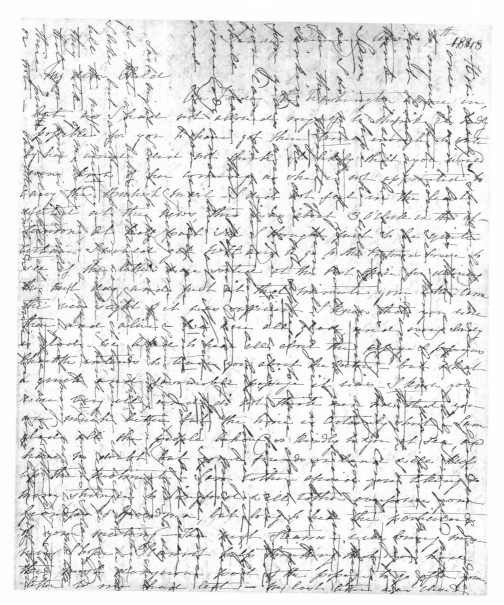

Cross-written letter from Charlotte to Lucy, dated April 9, 1848. Letters were sometimes written in two directions to save paper and postage costs. This eight-page letter was "crosswritten" in two different ink colors.

But in December 1848 came the startling news to eastern America of the discovery of gold in California. The Kendalls, like everyone else in the city of New York, were caught up in the excitement, which became hysterical as the days passed. When Joseph Kendall declared that he too would go to California to make his fortune, and when Mr. Harry offered to loan him the money for the venture, Mrs. Kendall wrote to England that Lucy must think of returning. The news from California was to change all their lives. But even Mrs. Kendall did not know at the time what tremendous changes the future held for all of them.

NOTES

1. The following are the entries found in the New York City Directories of that era: 1837: "Kendall, Joseph–Paints–308 Grand St. (H–65 Eldridge St.)" 1850–51: "Kendall, Joseph–painter, 24 Market St." 1851–52: "Kendall, Joseph–24 Market St." Additional notes made by Florence Herrick Requa in 1935 explain the locations of these addresses: 24 Market St. was at the "corner of Henry St., which is near Division and runs from Oliver to Grand," 65 Eldridge St. was "near Division," and "Grand St. runs from 78 Varick East to East River."
2. Newbury is twenty miles south of Oxford on the road to Southampton.
3. First edition, 1857.
4. See Carl C. Cutler, *Greyhounds of the Sea: The Story of the American Clipper Ship* (New York: Halcyon House, 1930). Two years after Lucy's voyage, on June 22, 1850, the *Southampton* with Capt. E. E. Morgan at the helm made a record-setting Atlantic crossing of thirteen days.

The illustration of Ventnor (p.19) is from *Nelson's Pictorial Guide Books for Tourists,* "The Isle of Wight, Part Fourth: Ventnor, the Undercliff, and Back of Island" (London, Edinburgh, and New York: T. Nelson and Sons, n.d.).

GOLD IN CALIFORNIA

Pencil sketch of San Francisco Bay by Joseph Kendall, October 1849.

By the middle of January 1849, it had definitely been settled that Joseph Kendall was going to California "for Gold." His wife immediately wrote to her parents in England telling of the momentous decision and again urging Lucy's return. The excitement, rumors, hopes, and plans buzzing about in New York are well portrayed in Charlotte's letters to her parents. Beyond the pervasive excitement of the news of gold and the final decision of Joseph to go after it, there was much indecision in Charlotte's situation. On the one hand, she had hopes for Joseph's better health and the wealth he might bring back. But, on the other hand, she had the responsibilities of Annie, the declining business, and her household of boarders to maintain. Not only was she facing these difficulties with Joseph gone, but in the event she should follow him, she would need to dispose of her responsibilities also. A future with so many indefinite possibilities at times seemed overwhelming. All this, and Lucy, her confidante, her moral support, was in far England and seemed reluctant to leave her adoring circle of family and suitors in the dead of winter.

Charlotte's appreciation of the close relationship her parents had with Lucy at two critical periods in her life—during her formative years and now at a time when she was gravely ill—is eloquently conveyed in this letter:[1]

From Charlotte Paxton Kendall to Wm. and Anne Paxton at Langford, Bicester, England.

24 Market Street
New York, U.S.A.

19th January, 1849

My dear Father and Mother:
. . . I expect my dear Lucy will be just on the eve of leaving you when this arrives, and a sad trial I know it will be to her, and not an easy separation to you, confided as she has been to you at some of the most tender and important periods of her life. And even her life itself has now, I quite believe, been preserved by flying to your quiet covert for rest and strength. The anxiety you have many times felt about her health and safety has endeared her more to you than anything else could. . . .
I am glad when I think of you at Langford, that you are not likely to suffer by the changes and turmoil that are agitating the rest of the world, and that even these exciting tidings of the inexhaustible gold mines will not move you, as they are creating such a stir in the population of this part of the world . . . such has never been heard of before. Newspapers are full of maddening intelligence, and private information confirms the statements that are drawing thousands and tens of thousands in desperation to get there. In every part of New York, and it is the same in other cities, companies, associations, and little parties have been and are organizing for mining in California.
The ships are becoming scarce, having been rapidly bought up for these expeditions, and now the people are going overland in large numbers together, for protection. But it is a fearful undertaking this way, as they cannot take the necessary quantity of provisions to sustain them while there, as there has already been great suffering for want of food and plenty of gold could not buy it. Even the natives

had not cultivated their lands as much as usual, so that there has not been enough. Now there is food enough, but it will be very dear.

All ships are taking immense cargoes of flour, etc., besides enough for their own people, sufficient for eighteen months or two years. All sorts of implements, hastily manufactured—wooden houses to be hooked together when they get there, tents, wheelbarrows, machines for breaking rocks, and sifting gold, ploughs, mills, weapons of all sorts, lots of useful things; also ornamental rubbish for sale.

Joseph has been set on going if possible, from the first, but so many impediments existed that although he did not give it up there seemed no probability of accomplishing his wish. However, I think now that he will manage it.

I have wished all the time to go with him, but see that if I persist in it he cannot go at all. The expense, which is a monstrous item for one, would be out of the question for us all. I should have to take Annie, and would not like to leave Lucy; then there are no women going, and no habitations for them at present, if they did.

So, with conditions existing as they are, Joseph is going without the rest of us. He will make one of a company of thirty, who will take provisions and all necessities for two years. In one year I should hear from him, and if it should seem best, go to him; but I think this would not be the case, and he would come back here, and I have no doubt, if he lives, will bring a rich reward for his trip. Then I should pay our debts in England, and perhaps see you all again. . . .

Then there is the expectation of Joseph's health being better. For a long time he has been ailing and has been constantly advised to attempt some other business, which, however, has not seemed practicable, having never given the least attention to anything in his life beside, and this venture would accomplish having a new business and the change he needs. I shall look for him back with invigorated health and thousands of dollars worth of gold.

In the meantime I shall try to go on with the painting business with the help of one man, and reduce our expenses to the lowest

possible sum; and with Lucy's earnings (from [teaching] music) and
the trifle the business will yield I shall try to get through the year. I
do dread it a little, but shall keep looking forward.

After that I think there will be no occasion for Joseph to work at
the painting, or for dear Lucy to teach music. She must not let anything but illness prevent her from returning with Captain Hovey. I
have given her the reasons for wanting her to return now, and she
has told me that you would pay her passage back or I should have
made some arrangement with Captain Hovey, though that would be
difficult indeed to do. . . .

21st January,

We have heard that the rush to California is quite as great from
Liverpool and other English ports as it is from this side.

Joseph has borrowed the money and will leave us to scramble
along day by day as we can in his absence, but I think we shall not
die of starvation in this bounty. In one year, if Joseph lives, we shall
know our destiny, and I am full of bright visions such as never filled
my mind before, because at the best of times I have never thought of
much beyond a living, but now I feel confident of being well-off.

The Government is about to take steps to prevent foreigners from
landing in California, at least with the intention of mining, but
Joseph is a citizen and is privileged to have just as much as he can get.
So thousands from other countries [also] will think, and as the facili-
ties for landing are great everywhere and the gold regions so extensive
there will be but little chance of preventing them from coming.

There is to be a mint established directly at San Francisco. At
present there is a man-of-war stationed there acting as a bank, trans-
mitting the money to these parts.

Our George[2] ought to go, and come here first, and go in one of
these regular American ships. The sum for the whole voyage there
and back, with a share of vessel, provisions for two years, equal

share in any company, possessing all the apparatus for mining, and making you one of the interests of the company is $250.

The disadvantages of going by land are chiefly the impossibility of taking sufficient provisions, and of having to walk many miles or ride on mules, either of which would be almost killing for Joseph.

They could make the journey in two months, through Mexico or across the Isthmus of Darien [formerly a name that was interchangeable with that of Panama], but would have no home when they get there. But going round the Cape they will be five or six months, and the ship will be a home when they get there, and bring them back when they are ready to come.

If our George does go, he must not start from England with less than a hundred pounds. If he misses this chance he never ought to look beyond a stone pit again. We have several plans as to the best way of getting over the time till Joseph returns. One is to sell everything we have in the world, do the best we can with the proceeds, and go into the country and board in a cheap way. This is not settled, but when it is you shall know. But I shall not move a step in anything till Lucy arrives; she must come now, or I do not know what I shall do. I do not mean that I want her to work for me, because if we go into the country she will not have to work at all, but I must have my children with me. And I know although she will grieve to leave you all, that she would not be happy to stay any longer. Will you tell her to bring every scrap and bit of clothing that she has because she will have nothing more till her father comes back from California. When he does come we mean to pay all our debts in England, and you, my dear Father, of course. He must be successful enough for that, for we know beyond a doubt of the abundance of wealth there is for all who will go for it. Rich as well as poor are going. But all my friends, as well as Dr. McClay, say that the voyage will set Joseph entirely to rights, and that he could not continue in his business without seriously increasing this evil. Besides this is the best and as well the last chance for making a good lot of money. . . .

Lucy must not be surprised if her Pa should be gone when she gets here. If he goes with the party that at present seems most desirable, he will. I mean to get him a lot of warm things and a buffalo skin to wear round the Cape, as it will be cold there at the time he reaches that point. Most of the time it will be hot enough, except for a short time at starting. He will pass through the torrid zone four times before he gets back, that is if he comes that (same) way. But a great many intend to sell their ships when they have done with it, and come home the nearer way, by the Isthmus, which will occupy only two months. How glad I shall be to see you and how glad you will all be to hear that he is come back and has lots of gold.

. . . Our business has been very bad the last ten months. This spring Joseph expected it would be better and that he should have the steamboat work again. He gave great satisfaction last year, and he was desirous that he should do them again. The Company, however, is at loggerheads and perhaps will not have them done at all, or if they do it will be in a cheap inferior manner.

I shall be very busy now for the next month, after that I shall write again. We have a lodger, a lawyer, who reduces our present expenses a little, but I shall be glad when Lucy comes that I may be more at liberty to live, anyhow. Captain Ferrier has just come in and they are making arrangements about California. He is not going himself, but he is the general friend and advisor of many who are.

The government has sent troops there to preserve peace, for there is no law yet, but all these gold-seekers, or at least a large majority, are well-conducted people. The worst sort of the population cannot get there.

Tell Lucy not to dread the passage back. It is a safe, first-rate ship and excellent kind captain.

Love to you and all under your care. I am your affectionate daughter,

Charlotte.

The euphoric atmosphere of New York being one to buoy the spirits, Charlotte always kept "looking forward": toward Lucy's return, to Joseph's better health, and to wealth that would more than meet their debts and a comfortable living. Though she believed that Joseph's health would return with the fresh salt air of the voyage, there was a long separation to face and uncertainty as to when or how he would return or if she would go to him.

As she had promised in the above letter, a month later Charlotte Kendall wrote to her parents again. The second letter shows that Lucy was still reluctant to return, and that Mrs. Kendall—for the moment—resigned herself to the continued separation as she helped Joseph to his departure.

24 Market Street
February 18th, 1849

My dear Father:

I received your letter a few days ago and certainly appreciate all your kind actions and intentions to my dear Lucy, and as a further proof that I do, am quite willing for her to remain with you for an indefinite time, if she has not on the spur of my last letter already left Langford. It was not that I was not conscious of her present comforts and safety, that I was anxious for her to return, nor was it an uncontrollable desire to see her—for the wish to see her should yield to her welfare—but it was the conviction that this would be the best for herself (I mean in regard to her own business employments), not contemplating at all that you would wish to keep her permanently with you, with such a little flock as you have around you. Then, the fact of her father going to California so soon seemed to stamp the impression on my mind that she ought at once to secure the remaining patronage of her friends—however, if she is not on the way home, she may with my consent stay with you.

Joseph's arrangements are made to leave New York about the last week in this month or the first of next. He is going in a company of sixty, a good many of which he knows. It is called the "Island City

Lucy Kendall, from a daguerreotype taken in England before her last voyage across the Atlantic Ocean, 1849.

Mining and Trading Association." Their Constitution and regulations are registered, and are, it is said, excellent. I should like to send you the particulars, if I have an opportunity. The bark "Canton," a beautiful and nearly new vessel, belongs to the company. Captain Ferrier is making the chief arrangements for the ship. His nephew is one of them. There is a Doctor going who is also one of them. You can form no idea of the time and trouble of organizing and getting out one of these expeditions. The company is legally bound together for one year after their arrival at San Francisco. If they choose to disband then, the vessel is to be sold and all the proceeds divided; but during the year that they work together, there will be a division of the proceeds every month, reserving a fifth to keep them together. The share of each member is to go on in cases of illness or death precisely the same—but I cannot tell you a hundredth part of the fixed articles of the Company.

Joseph was determined if possible to go from the first, but there did not seem the least chance for some time. He is to give an understood and reasonable proportion of his earnings for the sum he has borrowed for his membership and outfit.

Dr. McClay, our doctor, says that the voyage will restore him to health. It will do a great deal, certainly, if it does, for he is very much out of order now, although he is in pretty good spirits.

Our business is a little better, just now; most people tell me that it will be better when I conduct it, but really I can have but little to do with it; however I have great confidence in the ability and honesty of the man (Harper) who is to superintend it during Joseph's absence.

Fondest love to dear Mother. I shall write again soon.
Your affectionate daughter,

Charlotte.

Joseph Kendall himself wrote to his daughter of the intended voyage. This letter has been published in full in *A Landsman's Voyage*, and is here only given in part.

New York
Sunday January 10th, 1849

My dear Lucy:

How often have I longed to see you, and . . . Oh! what delight should I have if I could . . . press you to my bosom, ere I leave this city for a far-off distant land! But I shall not, I fear, see you for many a long day. Yet I trust my going will be beneficial to my health and also for the good of all of us in the end. If I live I am determined to do all in my power to get the thing so much wanted, which is GOLD!

I shall have to go, dearest, around the Horn, and if you refer to the map of the world you will then see what a way it is, being nearly eighteen thousand miles and nearly your antipodes.[3] Fancy it! Poor Pa! . . . Two years is certainly a long time to be away from your side, and if I had not seen so many ups and downs I should not have ventured so far.

I will save all the gold I can, and if I get hold of any diamonds, I will keep them also. One good thing is, our ship is our own, and when we get up the Sacramento River we intend erecting a wooden house which we will take with us. This will be better for our health than sleeping, as thousands do, on the bare ground and having only a tent to cover them. . . .

Two weeks later he wrote further:

Sunday evening, 23rd

I have, my dear child, read your affectionate and, to me, delight-ful and sensible letter. I had some difficulty in reading some of it. My eyes are not as good as formerly, and being also much affected caused the tears to roll fast as I read it.

What a dear child you are! Your Grandpa did not overrate you when he expressed such strong language about you. I hope you will endeavor to cheer their declining years and make their last days truly happy. Your poor Ma will have enough to contend with, that's certain, yet I think will do well. . . .

How very kind they all are to you my dear! But who is this Mr. Turner? How kindly he also seems to be. Is it anything besides friendship, or what? I love everybody who behaves well to my Lucy.

There is lots of news daily about California. I wish we were there and at work. We have all kinds of mechanics with us, which is a good thing—carpenters, ship-carpenters, smiths, painters, masons, etc. . . .

My dear, I shall have to encounter, I guess, people of all grades and tribes and tongues, from every clime—what a motley group! It would be like Babel. We shall soon have to make rules and laws, for there are roaming desperadoes who rob and murder for the gold which others collect. The better class of people have hung up four-teen in the Lynch-law system. This would be the only way to put down such fellows. If George [Paxton] comes tell him to buy a good English rifle. . . . I hope sincerely that he may come. It will improve health and spirits and make him another human being. . . .

Mr. Baker's nephew from New Brunswick has bought a schooner, and thirty men have joined a company and paid $600 each, and sailed off for the gold regions. What a multitude have gone from this city already! When will they stop? I know not. There are, up to now, twenty-one vessels fitting for California, probably many more. . . .

I hope you, my darling, will enjoy much health and comfort till we meet again, which I hope will be, in reality, never to part till death. From your loving father

Joseph Kendall.

Although Kendall had expected to sail from New York as early as March sixth, the *Canton* did not actually leave the harbor until the last day of that month, one thing and another delaying the company. It was months later that he commenced another letter to Lucy, telling of the actual departure:

South Atlantic Ocean
June 8th

. . . I must give you a rough statement since we left New York. I left on Thursday, about 12 o'clock, after the painful but hasty farewells of my dear wife and sweet Annie. God bless them! I never felt anything more keenly in my life!

Well, dear, a steamboat towed us into the North River, and there [we] dropped anchor. Many of the company left the vessel and proceeded into the city, but my feelings were so acute I dared not go back to Market Street, much as I longed to do so.

I slept aboard with about ten or twelve others. But, oh, what thoughts came over me! What a wretched night it was to me, thinking that I was leaving my dearest to encounter difficulties and without anything like enough money! Oh, my darling, I cannot write! May the Lord be her comfort and protection till I return, and carry her through all her sorrows.

I received a note in the morning by darling Annie and Mr. Harry who came early with Captain Ferrier. Your Ma was pained very much because I had not returned, but I knew if I did it would quite unnerve me, so I was determined not to do so.

Annie brought me a few nice apples and a small spyglass—the very thing I wanted, and which I shall always prize. She also brought me a few candies, in addition to a quantity she brought a few days before I left, all of which lasted for about two months ere they were all gone. What a treat such little things are at sea! Your Mama also put up about one dozen pots of preserved quinces, which were excellent, and I eat a little when I feel the need for something sweet. . . .

And so "dear Papa" was on his way to great adventure.

Pencil sketch by Joseph Kendall entitled "A Vessel aground on the San Wakin [Joaquin]."

Before leaving New York, Kendall had turned his business over to his partner, Harper. Mrs. Kendall and Annie he had commended to Mr. Harry, but when he had finally sailed on the 31st of March, 1849, he went without knowing whether Lucy would return to America or not. Many ties, notably romantic, seemed to be keeping her in England. Almost immediately after his departure, however, Harper proved quite incapable of running the business alone,[4] and Mrs. Kendall wrote in distress to Lucy, begging her to return to New York to help with family finances.

It was not until late in the summer (August 1849) that Lucy was able to sail for New York in the care of Captain Morgan of the *Southampton*. She was a first-class passenger on the sailing ship, travelling in the Captain's friendly care. It was to be her fifth and last trip across the Atlantic. Shortly before her father had sailed for California in March 1849, he had become a naturalized citizen, which automatically made his wife and daughters citizens as well. Lucy would live no more in "dear England."

Mrs. Kendall met her daughter at the South Street dock. Lucy went back to teaching music which, with money from Mr. Harry's board, was for some time the only means of family income.

The first letter that the Kendalls received from Joseph, to say that he had actually arrived in California, came by way of Panama late in November. On the 15th of October he had been able to write Lucy briefly that he was in "The Bay off San Francisco, Upper California." Contrary to the Company's expectations on leaving New York, he said that they were not going up the Sacramento River. Rather, he wrote ". . . I go to the mines, darling Lucy, tomorrow. My destination is Stockton, up the San Wakin [Joaquin] River, about one hundred miles from where we are now living. . . ."

They had been more than six months aboard the *Canton*. The passengers had landed only once in that long tedious time, at Chatham Island in the Galapagos, although they had sighted other islands of the Pacific. As he wrote in his journal, and in letters to Lucy and to others, his drawing and sketching had been his only pleasure. He had not actually recovered his health, or spirits, until they had rounded the Horn, but thereafter he was restored. Somehow, too, he had learned to adapt himself to the often uncongenial companions on the bark. "We have some of the most horrid, swearing, spitting characters aboard I have *ever* seen," he commented. His drawings, he added, he would send on as soon as possible.

Soon Joseph Kendall sent his drawings and the journal of the voyage, made en route to California, back to his family in New York. (Except for one brief letter, all of his communications from Stockton were, unfortunately, destroyed early this century.)

It is possible to follow a bit of his first three years in California from the sketchbook he kept there, and from a few other sources. Upon arriving on the West Coast, he made two rather crude sketches of the Bay of San Francisco; the first shows the entrance to the bay "with fort at the mouth of the ditto." The other is of the inner bay. He also sketched the Baptist Chapel in Washington Street in the very new city itself. This was included, no doubt, to reassure his wife that there were, after all, some Christian influences at work in this outlandish community.

The *Canton* only anchored off the city for eight days. Arriving at San Francisco on the 8th of October, they set sail for Stockton on the San Joaquin on the 16th. Joseph included several sketches of the voyage up river, which was not without incident. One sketch shows "our Pilot"—peaceful, reading a book under a sail. The next shows "A vessel aground on the San Wakin"—undoubtedly the *Canton,* for next is shown "A part of the Cargo ashore to lighten the bark *Canton,* in the toles [tules]." There is some evidence that they were obliged to ask for a tow from one of the river steamboats already plying inland California waters. With high tide they floated free again and the next sketch shows "The cargo on Shore at Stockton in the Toles."

At Stockton, Kendall observed the new and strange life in the Spanish California countryside. "A Californian" is recorded by his pencil—an Indian perhaps, mounted on a wiry mustang and whirling a lariat. He also sketches another native striding down Stockton's crude streets in poncho, sombrero, slashed trousers, huge spurs, as he smokes a "seegar" and swings a firkin in either hand.

Probably Kendall, with other members of the Island City Mining Association, went to the mines immediately after his arrival in Stockton in October 1849. One sketch in his book shows "An exact representation of a piece of Gold found in the Mokelany [Mokelumne] River belonging to Wm. Tyler." But if he did go to the "diggings," the winter rains soon drove him back to Stockton. "I dread the rain and the mud with which I shall have to contend again unless I make a goodly sum," he wrote Lucy. And we have no record of his finding any reward in the placers. "Old Williams has made four thousand dollars and 'vamoose' to New York by last steamer. Also Hutton has made a lucky hit of about six thousand dollars. The others have so far made scarcely anything," he wrote later. In December he was painting "Mr. Dickenson's Hotel" in Stockton. And from then on, apparently, he returned to his old occupation of painting and decorating. In the summer of 1850 he was again painting steamboats, this time the steamer *El Dorado*. It is improbable that he ever again went to the mines.

Canvas sack, 3½ x 6 inches, which held the gold dust sent from California by Joseph Kendall in 1850 to his wife in New York City. Mrs. Kendall "called for the dust at the Express Office and took it around the corner to the mint," where it was coined for her.

An old bill for the painting at the hotel, entered in the back of his sketchbook, gives some interesting details. "For Mr. Dickenson's Painting at Hotel. The Bar Room, & sashes upstairs etc." One item, on January 1, shows that Kendall was "Marbling etc. from seven in the morning till 2 o'clock next morn." Kendall was doing his usual careful work, "five coats for marbling" and he was making $16 to $20 a day. This particular bill was for $270. "By cash on account $20. Bal. in Dust $250." He must also have collected gold dust to send home shortly: one small canvas sack, with marks of sealing wax still on it, by which gold dust was sent to his wife, is still in existence. Sent by Adams Express, it was addressed to "Mrs. C. Kendall, N. York," and in the corner is stated the amount enclosed, "$645.23." Lucy used to tell her daughters how "dear Mamma took the dust around the corner to the mint and had it coined." Lucy also cherished a coin sent her by her father. "A half eagle, gold without alloy," stamped 1849. Years later, she gave it to her oldest granddaughter the day that she, six months old, was christened.

Receiving gold dust was a very exciting business, and Mrs. Kendall was quick to send the word on to her parents. In all probability she also paid off the debt they owed her father, for when summer came, William Paxton wrote jubilantly of Joseph Kendall's good fortune in a letter to his sister-in-law (soon to be Lady Paxton). "Joseph Kendall is at California, rolling in gold dust. He has sent one bagful to his wife, and gives a flattering account of his prospects."

Back in Stockton, Joseph Kendall soon established himself. In the sole letter extant from that city, written in August 1850, he speaks of "my store." As early as March he had advertised in the *Stockton Times:*

Joseph Kendall
House, Sign, and Ornamental Painter,
Gilding, Graining and Paper Hanging,
Ceilings decorated in fresco.
All orders executed with the utmost dispatch.

In his sketchbook he notes much in the growing city of Stockton: the Stockton House and the Phoenix Hotel; Grobot & Cie., Patissier, Restaurateur; E. D. Prentice, Groceries, Provisions. The last place, a very crude, barnlike structure, he called, "My present residence and place of abode." He also drew a half a dozen forty-niners, one eating with his knife! These portraits are his best sketches; the others, though cruder, are interesting historically.

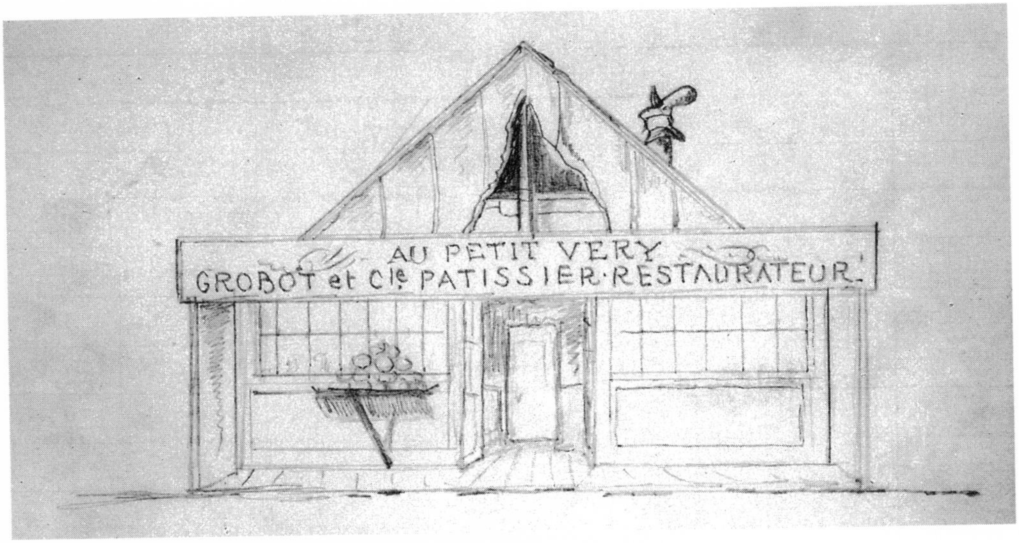
AU PETIT VERY
GROBOT et Cie PATISSIER·RESTAURATEUR.

Pencil sketch by Joseph Kendall of a restaurant in Stockton, 1850.

He was also taking an active interest in his surroundings. He "now knew much Spanish," and he had also become aware of the Chinese, speaking of a vessel that had come from China and buying Chinese objects to send to his family. In December 1850 he served on a jury in Stockton. As time passed, he became more settled in California, but it was not until 1852 that it was definitely decided that he would not return east: his wife and daughters, with Mr. Harry, would instead come west to him.

NOTES

1. This and the next letter of Mrs. Kendall to her parents were given to Lucy by the Paxtons at Langford, and cherished by her until her death in far-distant California. They have been published in part only in *A Landsman's Voyage*.
2. George Paxton, younger brother of Charlotte Paxton Kendall.
3. Webster's definition of "antipodes" is a place on the other side of the earth. British usage meant New Zealand or Australia.
4. In spite of Joseph Kendall's absence, the New York City Directories continued to have listings for the business through 1850. After that date there was only a home address listed.

PASSAGE BY GOLD DUST

Pencil sketch by Joseph Kendall entitled "My present residence."

In New York, through 1850–51, Mrs. Kendall and her daughters lived quietly, awaiting what they expected would be Joseph's return. During his prolonged absence their young boarder, Mr. Harry, was a great support, not only to their morale but to their finances. Many a time, without the knowledge of his impractical friends, he paid a bill or met some obligation that might have been worrisome.

Without Lucy's small income from music lessons, Mrs. Kendall would have been sadly put to it, for Joseph's fortunes in Stockton blew hot and cold. His contributions to the family economy were uncertain. Twice he wrote that he had been "burned out" just when he expected to sell his store at a profit. These catastrophes he dismissed as a not uncommon occurrence in the mining towns, but they prevented his return. Each time, Joseph rebuilt and began his fortunes over again. As months passed, he began to speak of his family coming out to him.

Wild pioneer ways, he told them, were settling into more conservative ones in California, and money was to be made more easily than in New York. The climate was good, and if he moved to San Francisco, there was a "society" of decent women and churchgoing people. They would find the city by the Golden Gate a not unpleasant place to live—and at least in California there was "a good living" for them all. So what had seemed impossible began to seem plausible and the idea of joining Joseph slowly took shape in their minds.

Meanwhile, in December 1851, New York went wild with the excitement of welcoming the Hungarian hero Louis Kossuth,[1] and according him such a reception as they had given no foreigner since Lafayette's triumphal return of a quarter-century before. There was a parade, cheered by thousands, in his honor. The Hungarian with his four colonels— Perczel, Hasman, Berczenzey, and Asboth—led the procession, and Lucy and Annie, amid the cheering throngs along the way, thrilled in sympathy with Hungary and "Freedom." The parade swept by, but Lucy little realized that one of the Hungarians would cross their path in a more informal way.

A few months later the "dust" arrived from Joseph Kendall to pay for their passage, and it was finally decided that the three women, with Mr. Harry, would go west to California. Tickets were purchased on one of the new Vanderbilt steamers to Nicaragua. But, before their departure, the papers were filled with the news of the explosion of *The North American*, one of the Vanderbilt steamboats, with a great loss of life, and Mrs. Kendall declared that the terrors of Cape Horn were preferable to the risk of being blown to "Kingdom Come." Family tradition says that she went herself to Commodore Vanderbilt and asked for the return of their passage money. The Commodore replied, "Mrs. Kendall, I would do it for no one but you." And he complied.

Through Mr. Harry, Mrs. Kendall was able to buy passage for them all on a freight vessel that only carried eight passengers, sailing via Cape Horn. The ship *Josephine*[2] seemed a stout little craft, and seaworthy to inexperienced eyes. As it turned out, they would have done better to have trusted the steamboat, for the cargo the *Josephine* would carry was incredibly explosive.

All three sat for their daguerreotypes to give to friends whom they felt they would never see again. All Lucy's friends must write in her friendship

Charlotte Kendall, 1852.

Annie Kendall, 1852.

46

The Portsmouth Journal, February 28, 1852

Fast as one ship goes another new one appears at one of our wharves; each vieing with the other in claims either to model, strength or beauty.—The above ship *Josephine,* of 947 tons, was built at the yard of Samuel Hanscom, Jr., in Eliot, about three miles above Portsmouth Bridge, for Gen. Joseph Andrews of Salem. She is a well built ship, and although an effort is made to avoid all gaudy appearance, she is truly handsome, and her proportions are so good as to deceive the eye in estimating her size.

She is built of the New Hampshire white oak, which like the Granite Hills, is famous the world over. She is 170 feet on deck, 36 feet wide, 22 feet 6 inches deep; has two entire decks and a full poop 84 feet long, and a house between the fore and main mast, 34 feet for offices, galley, &c., and a top gallant forecastle for the crew.—The cabin is the largest we recollect having visited, being 45 feet in length. The accommodations for passengers are excellent. The cabin is finished in a rich but not gaudy manner, and furnished in Mr. S. M. Dockum's usual good style. The veneering of the cabin was done by Mr. A. T. Joy [A cabinetmaker at 42 Market St.] Portsmouth, and the joiner work by Mr. S. Amos Trott [Penhallow Street]; the painting was done by Mr. L. A. Bruce [Market Street].

The *Josephine* is to be commanded by William Jameson, of Saco, under whose superintendence she was built. She will sail early next week, probably for New Orleans. Success to these children of the Piscataqua.

Charlotte Kendall probably read this favorable notice in The Portsmouth Journal, *and after the Vanderbilt steamer blew up, purchased passage on the* Josephine.

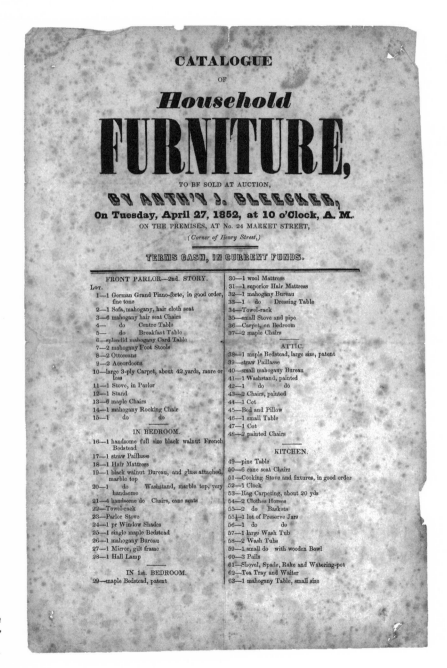

CATALOGUE

OF

Household

FURNITURE,

TO BE SOLD AT AUCTION,

BY ANTH'Y J. BLEECKER,

On Tuesday, April 27, 1852, at 10 o'Clock, A. M.

ON THE PREMISES, AT No. 24 MARKET STREET,

(Corner of Henry Street,)

TERMS CASH, IN CURRENT FUNDS.

FRONT PARLOR—2nd. STORY.

Lot.

1—1 German Grand Piano-forte, in good order, fine tone
2—1 Sofa, mahogany, hair cloth seat
3—6 mahogany hair seat Chairs
4—   do   Centre Table
5—   do   Breakfast Table
6—splendid mahogany Card Table
7—2 mahogany Foot Stools
8—2 Ottomans
9—2 Accordeons
10—large 3-ply Carpet, about 42 yards, more or less
11—1 Stove, in Parlor
12—1 Stand
13—6 maple Chairs
14—1 mahogany Rocking Chair
15—1   do   do

IN BEDROOM.

16—1 handsome full size black walnut French Bedstead
17—1 straw Paillasse
18—1 Hair Mattress
19—1 black walnut Bureau, and glass attached, marble top
20—1   do   Washstand, marble top, very handsome
21—4 handsome do   Chairs, cane seats
22—Towel-rack
23—Parlor Stove
24—1 pr Window Shades
25—1 single maple Bedstead
26—1 mahogany Bureau
27—1 Mirror, gilt frame
28—1 Hall Lamp

IN 1st. BEDROOM.

29—maple Bedstead, patent

30—1 wool Mattress
31—1 superior Hair Mattress
32—1 mahogany Bureau
33—1   do   Dressing Table
34—Towel-rack
35—small Stove and pipe
36—Carpet, on Bedroom
37—2 maple Chairs

ATTIC.

38—1 maple Bedstead, large size, patent
39—straw Paillasse
40—small mahogany Bureau
41—1 Washstand, painted
42—1   do   do
43—2 Chairs, painted
44—1 Cot
45—Bed and Pillow
46—1 small Table
47—1 Cot
48—2 painted Chairs

KITCHEN.

49—pine Table
50—6 cane seat Chairs
51—Cooking Stove and fixtures, in good order
52—1 Clock
53—Rag Carpeting, about 20 yds
54—2 Clothes Horses
55—2   do   Baskets
55½—1 lot of Preserve Jars
56—1   do   do
57—1 large Wash Tub
58—2 Wash Tubs
59—1 small do   with wooden Bowl
60—3 Pails
61—Shovel, Spade, Rake and Watering-pot
62—Tea Tray and Waiter
63—1 mahogany Table, small size

Handbill for the auction of the Kendalls' household goods.

album, as they had done in Charlotte Kendall's in Bicester twenty years before. And as the large grand pianoforte was to be sold, a small upright was purchased to take its place in their San Francisco home. This, with a mahogany card table, the piano stool, some Queen Anne chairs from Bicester, and all the musical instruments, was all they would take to California, except their personal possessions. Lucy kept one of the auction handbills among her papers until her death.

There were a great many calls made and received before their departure, for the Kendalls left many friends, and they must take letters from the Baptist church, too. Only a few days before they left, Lucy received a farewell letter from their old friend Rev. Octavius Winslow in England. Of the final closing of the paint shop, the farewells to old Winnie, school friends, music pupils, church members, there is no record. Lucy herself tells the story of the voyage in the journal that follows.

NOTES

1. Louis (or Lajos) Kossuth had led the unsuccessful Hungarian rebellion of 1848–49. When uprisings broke out in the Austrian Empire in 1848, the Hungarians were led by Kossuth. When he refused independence to the minorities living under his rule, the Austrians, with the help of Russia, regained control. After being exiled in Turkey for a short time, he toured the United States, being hailed as the "Hungarian George Washington."

2. Cutler, *Greyhounds of the Sea*. The *Josephine* was built by Samuel Hanscom, Jr., in Eliot, Maine, its owner Gen. Joseph Andrews, Salem; the ship burned in St. Louis Harbor, Mauritius, in June 1859.

Inside cover and first page of Lucy Kendall Herrick's journal.

Voyage to California
~ 1852 ~

On the 25th of April we had a sale of all superfluous furniture, and soon after the rest together with our luggage was shipped on board the Ship Josephine, bound for California — A long time passed however ere we started, delays of various kinds occurred and although we were thereby enabled to visit our friends, and take farewell of all that we held dear in New York, still long suspense had rendered us impatient and we gladly hailed the certain intelligence that we were to sail on the morning of the 25th of May, one month exactly since we had been ready and waiting — A Steamboat conveyed us to our ship which lay at anchor some distance from the dock — the morning seemed auspicious, and nothing but the sad thought of the final parting shed gloom around us — we pass over those moments of grief, when the heartstrings are strained to the utmost; when the eyes refuse to shed tears of relief: and emotions far too strong to describe choke utterance — the last hand is shaken — the last kiss given — the last look taken — yes we are parted! — for what different scenes — a family bound on a long and perilous voyage to a strange land to a strange people, they to join the family circle, and enjoy the comforts of home and land — Nevertheless the same hand that shields us on dry land is present to protect on the mighty deep — shall we not trust Him whom the winds and the waves obey? — A brisk breeze sent us rapidly on and evening had commenced ere the distressing qualms of seasickness assailed us — then we were conquered! Of all

Lucy Kendall on the eve of her 1852 voyage.

Here in Lucy's own words we have a day-by-day account of her voyage to California—her delights, pursuits, and interests, including the anguish and fears brought on by storms at sea. She carried a small pocket diary to record thoughts during the day and at night copied the notes in the journal pictured above. Although the diary is transcribed in full, spelling and punctuation have been standardized.

On the <u>28th of April</u> we had a sale of all superfluous furniture and soon after, the rest—together with our luggage—was sent on board the ship "Josephine," bound for California. A long time elapsed, however, ere we started; delays of various kinds occurred and although we were thereby enabled to visit our friends and take farewell of all we held dear in New York, still long suspense had rendered us impatient, and we gladly hailed the certain intelligence that we were to sail on the morning of the <u>25th of May</u>, one month exactly since we had been ready and waiting.

A steamboat conveyed us to the ship which lay at anchor some distance from the dock. The morning dawned auspiciously and nothing but the sad thought of the final parting shed gloom around us. We pass over those moments of pain when the heartstrings are strained to the utmost; when the eyes refuse to shed tears of relief; and emotions far too strong to describe choke utterance. The last hand is shaken, the last kiss given, the last look taken—yes, we are parted!—for what different scenes—<u>we</u>, a family bound on a long and perilous voyage to a strange land and a stranger people; <u>they</u> to join the family circle and enjoy the comforts of home and land. Nevertheless, the same hand that shields us on dry land is present to protect us on the mighty deep. Shall we not trust Him whom the winds and waves obey?

The steamboat left us at Sandy Hook; a brisk breeze sent us rapidly on and evening had commenced ere the distressing qualms of seasickness had assailed us—then we were conquered! Of all the ills to which we poor human beings are subject, none can well exceed that of seasickness. Who can describe it? Who can portray the diminishing of every hope, the utter loathing of everything our senses could grasp, the entire giving up of one's entire self to perfect, absolute despair! This is the effect and such were our feelings during the first few days of our voyage.

Our ship contains 42 individuals; namely, Captain Jameson and 8 cabin passengers: Mr. East, Mr. John and George Waterson, and their friend Mr. Hezekiah Cole, all three mechanics; Mrs. Waring, Mrs. Kendall and two daughters; the 2 mates, 20 sailors, 2 cooks, steward and stewardess; six boys before the mast; carpenter and a fine large Newfoundland dog; also about 15 dozen fowls, several turkeys, sheep, pigs, and, last but not least, Annie's 2 canaries. Our breakfast hour is 8—dinner 1—tea 6. The man at the helm has a bell which he strikes every half hour, until he has struck 8, when he begins with one again. This is to mark the "watch" of the sailors—4 hours being one "watch." Each time the helmsman strikes, a man at the bow or head of the vessel strikes in echo. Everything has to be done punctually and in order at sea. We have about six months before us, we believe, to spend at sea.

Thursday, 27th. We are crossing the Gulf Stream, the wind high, the weather tempestuous. Towards night the wind increased. Captain Jameson was sitting near the helm when a rope from the "spanker boom" suddenly caught him and, he being wholly unprepared, was taken overboard. It was quite dark; one rope only hung where he could possibly reach and this missed, he must be lost. Providentially he struck for it and seized it. Mr. John Waterson happened to see him and he was soon

on board again—a hairbreadth escape—. Darkness had now become
intense, distant thunder was heard, vivid flashes of lightning soon followed, almost blinding the poor men who had to work most vigorously.
The ship rolled heavily. This was a squall and such as are often met with
in this Gulf Stream. It is so called as it is a strong current of water (of a
much warmer temperature than other salt water) that flows from the
Gulf of Mexico. The peculiar temperature has never been accounted
for—probably the effect of some volcanic agency.

During the night all hands were up; all was wildness and confusion.
Fireballs played around the masts. Towards morning the gale somewhat
abated. I believe we all slept soundly below in happy unconsciousness of
the terrors around us.

Sunday 30th. A most delightful day. We are feeling somewhat
enlivened. Everything around looks bright, the sun shining clearly out of
a blue sky, while the glistening waves dance by us, "tipt" with white
foam. Our ship is in full sail, sailors in clean shirts, and a stillness reign-
ing around, which always to me seems to belong peculiarly to the
Sabbath. But we have no recognition of the Sabbath, beyond what I have
stated, no hymn of praise, no prayer for protection, no word of exhorta-
tion to cheer us on our way. This is a ship, although in every other way
desirable, that does not seem to profess the fear of God. Novel-reading
and an utter disregard for the day prevails. "The fool hath said in his
heart there is no God."[1] Yet we can silently breathe our wants to Him,
who will bow His ear when His people cry.

Monday 31st. A lovely day—fair wind—making good way on our course. Read "Uncle Tom's Cabin"—enough to arouse the indignation of the whole world as regards that bane of America, *slavery!*

Nothing could surpass the beauty of the evening; the moon with her brightest and gentlest beams rose in glory over the dark deep waters, while a few stars peeped out here and there amid distant clouds. The ocean, but just now wild and tumultuous, has sunk into a calm, and all seems peace. Oh, is it not on such a night that, in wonder and admiration, the heart silently acknowledges the being, goodness, and mercy of the Creator? "Are not the Heavens the work of His hands—the sea and all that is therein?" We stayed on deck late enjoying the scene.

Tuesday June 1st. We are now about 1,400 miles from New York. We shall soon be "on the line" if the wind continues favorable. We are all rapidly recovering from the effects of seasickness. Mr. East seems more himself. Mamma arranges the things in our rooms in case of stormy weather, while Annie once more resumes her wonted activity and is now set upon getting as many kinds of seaweed as she can. We obtained some today, but it was all of one kind. I have determined to work at sewing, etc., until dinnertime, draw and read until six, and walk and talk in the evening; thus my time being divided and fully occupied, it will pass quickly and pleasantly.

Our fellow passenger, Mrs. Waring, has suffered worse than any of us during our voyage so far. She is about 42 years old, has a liver complaint and a discontented disposition. Poor woman! All the world is against her, but Annie and I, being young, "don't feel it." Friends, she tells us, belong to the affluent and the prosperous; but, vice versa, enemies belong to the poor, depressed, and seasick. Surely such a complication of human woes, for so little a cause, has seldom been met with.

Mother Carey's chickens[2] follow in numbers at our stern, skimming along the wake, ready to catch anything eatable that may fall from the ship; if ever so small a substance, their sharp eyes instantly detect it. Flying fish have been seen today.

Our vessel has about <u>fifteen hundred kegs</u> of gunpowder on board, one keg being sufficient to blow us up, besides vitriol, turpentine, camphor, and alcohol. We are in rather a combustible plight, besides having, at the bottom of the ship, many tons of coal liable to spontaneous combustion. We were not a little distressed at this information, but we were ready to start before we knew of the cargo, or we would not have run the risk, and there was no alternative but to go.

<u>Wednesday June 2nd.</u> A fine day. Great quantities of orange-colored seaweed in beds floated by us on the blue waves whose tops were tipped with white foam.

Some fowls escaped on deck this morning, causing no little excitement, they being very much disposed to seek a watery grave in preference to being captured. I darned socks during the morning. Had a long talk with Mr. Cole and Mr. John Waterson in the afternoon. Mamma and Mr. Harry played chess. The evening air is delightful, soft, and balmy. We are able to sit on deck quite late. All is calm around, the vessel scarcely *moving. I write this sitting on a coil of rope by the side of the ship.*

<u>*Thursday June 3rd.*</u> *Every day is passed with so little variation that quite a time elapsed ere we could be satisfied as to what this day of the week was. Our weather continues delightful. I would not be in New York today for the world, the breeze is so refreshing. The sun will soon be vertical, our shadows are fast diminishing.*

Annie writes in her journal and enjoys herself very much. Mr. J. Waterson brought me a letter to read this morning, saying that he had received it from a young lady just before leaving. He is getting quite confidential! I am sorry he swears very much.

Many of those around us have traveled a great deal by sea and we glean a great deal of information from one another. We gain a good deal of information from one another on board. Several have traveled this way before—some to China; others to Brazil. Our steward is quite an intelligent man and has been to various quarters of the globe.

Mrs. Waring tells me today that Mr. Waring is very good about money—letting her have it, she means. She remarks this, on the strength of starting sewing a dress on deck. Our water is beginning to taste very bad. I saw a flying fish today for the first time.

This afternoon we met, and the Captain was able to "speak a Spanish brig," conveying troops to some far-off region. It came quite near and was crowded with soldiers; a mean-looking set of soldiers they appeared. Our flag was raised and drawn up and down, according to the formalities of seamen and answered in the same way. Longitude and latitude

Sketched on
~ The Josephine ~

were exchanged and after much waving of hats the courtesies were over and each ship proceeded on its way.

It is a mild and peaceful evening, betokening a still more beautiful sunset—would that I could describe the scene! The waters hushed and tranquil, the bright azure sky decked with mackerel clouds, while our ship glides softly onward.

Our Captain is a New England man, a regular "down Easter"—tall, rawboned, and sunburnt, with small piercing eyes and a peculiarly meaning and penetrating expression. From his mouth issues a cigar and he wears an old coat with a turn-down collar and a pair of old black trousers. Place him on his back on deck (as he is at present) with his feet elevated on a hen-coop, cigar tilted, a large Newfoundland dog beside him, and you have our Captain. He is quite obliging. All goes well and we have reason to be happy and thankful thus far.

<u>Friday June 4th.</u> Still fine, almost a dead calm, the sea placid and the clouds presenting a most beautiful appearance. Last night the moon rose like a ball of fire out of the ocean and as it shot upwards among the dark clouds, the effect baffles description. We walked the deck nearly an hour watching it. None can appreciate the beauties of a sunset or the rising of the moon who has not been to sea, particularly in the tropical regions.

We are making poor progress just now. One of the passengers who has served seven years before the mast in the United States Service has just been up the main top-gallant mast and cries out he "sees the trade *winds approaching." Trade winds are those winds which during certain seasons in certain latitudes blow steadily from one quarter and, of course, are favorable to commerce and are depended on by all seafaring men. I hope so, for the threat of continued calm seems to have a dispiriting effect on the Captain.*

Annie records many of the dialogues which take place between the passengers. Mr. John Waterson and I have had a remarkable argument on the subject of slavery, he being from Maryland, a slave state. He got quite excited; I offered him a peppermint-lozenge and we soon got into such a confused metaphysical state that we came out fast and firm on the North American Indians! Mr. East was almost convulsed at the way in which our assertions were supported. Now the Captain walks the deck again, cigar in mouth, and as he passes, coolly informs us drowning is an easy death—he has gone through it twice! The fowls have had some water today, poor things. They are on our deck and the noise they make is astonishing. I find myself getting some shades darker under the influence of a tropical sun, but if it does not get warmer, I am content.

<u>Saturday June 5th.</u> A glorious sunset.

<u>Sunday June 6th.</u> A fine day with a head wind. One ship in view. One of the sailors showed me how to tie some knots this morning.

<u>Monday June 7th.</u> We were awakened early this morning by hearing a strange voice which we soon discovered to belong to the Captain of an English vessel lying at our side. He had come aboard to buy some sea-biscuits and rice, which our Captain let him have. He was an old man,

friendly in his manner, and took a few hurried letters to our English friends, stating that he hoped to arrive in Liverpool in three weeks. During the day we have seen nine vessels.

I long to describe one of our unequalled sunsets. Could a painter delineate it, one who had not witnessed a tropical sunset would pronounce it exaggeration. The whole heavens appear in beautiful reflected shades, varying from the scarlet and gold that illumines the western horizon, to shades of violet, orange, and green, each seeming to vie with the other in beauty and spreading their radiance into the far east. And then the moon comes up, as if losing all timidity in these tropical regions, bursts forth from the heart of the ocean and, ascending 'midst the dark clouds, sheds abroad new brightness in lovely grandeur. Venus, too, casts a wide reflection on the sea, like another moon.

Tuesday June 8th. The weather is delightful, but during the morning we made very slow progress. A breeze arose towards evening, setting us off at a little brisker rate and from the constant pitching of the ship making us feel a little "qualmish." I felt the penetrating wind so that I sat on deck wrapped in the Captain's pea-jacket.

Wednesday June 9th. Every prospect of a dead calm; the sun very hot. One Belgian vessel in view. Sat hard at work all the morning. Slept for three hours this afternoon. Another splendid sunset, surpassing all the rest.

Thursday June 10th. A pleasant day. Annie was watching some sea-weed she had drawn up when she discovered a remarkable living creature, very small, about an inch and a half long, transparent, with six legs, on the whole resembling a miniature seahorse. She also found she had captured a young crab and a tiny sea-serpent. She takes great delight in watching for all sorts of curiosities.

It is a pity Mrs. Waring is so unlovable, as one's comfort at sea rests entirely on being agreeable to others, much more than on land.

I saw some black fish today. On the whole my time passes pleasantly. Besides "Uncle Tom's Cabin," I have read "Queechy" and am now reading "Ivanhoe."[3] The wind is low and we sail dreamily on.

Friday June 11th. A fresh breeze sprang up, carrying us on at a great rate.

We have been singing a little, both on deck and in the cabin . . . "When first I saw sweet Peggy, 'Twas on a market day."

This day a turkey flew overboard. The Captain ordered a boat to be lowered with four sailors and it was caught, but its feathers were so saturated with salt water it was deemed expedient to kill it and we had it for dinner. We have had poultry daily ever since we left New York. We have now about twelve dozen fowls and seven or eight turkeys. The Captain considers the turkeys worth thirty shillings each.

Saturday June 12th. Passed under a vertical sun.

Sunday June 13th. Contrary wind. Mr. J. Waterson caught a fish called bonito, which was cooked and pronounced good.

Monday June 14th. Fresh breeze blowing all day. Asked several persons the day of the month. Answers varied from the 10th to the 16th. Rather puzzled, but set right by a Dutch almanac.

Gave Mr. Cole, who was feeling poorly, a dose compounded of brandy and cream of tartar. Asked him if he felt better . . . answered "Not" . . . strange! I am always unfortunate in my prescriptions.

One of our boys fell down and hurt his back. The Captain intends doing something desperate to our old cook if he does not walk straighter—he is generally tipsy.

The vessel rolls very much today.

<u>Tuesday June 15th.</u> Last night was very rough and stormy. The sea was adverse (owing to the previous wind) while the present wind was in our favor and high. We had most sails set and the tremendous thumps aimed at our ship by the angry waves were calculated to shake the nerves of any landsman. But she bore it well, and came off some hundred miles the better for the conflict but oh, such tumbles have we experienced below! People and furniture rolling and tumbling, crockery breaking, doors creaking, and unaccountable noises on deck.

Annie made her bed on the floor and was so frightened that I launched myself out of my top berth—not being quite certain where I should alight—and lay down beside her. After much fuming and fussing for some time, we fell into an uneasy doze, from which I was awakened by a lurch of the ship which upset a tray of clothes on me and disconcerted me not a little. But we are traveling the right road, for surely the Path of Life is but alternate storms and calms through which we must sail ere we reach that land where the "weary are at rest."

Borne on the angry wave
My God, I look to Thee
Thou who alone canst save
Behold us on the sea!

The clouds are dark above,
The waters roar around
Preserve us with Thy love,
In Thee may we be found.

Oh Thou alone canst hush the deep
And bid its fury stay—
Canst safely keep us while we sleep
And guide us on our way.

How, during this restless night, have my thoughts wandered to those I love, far far off!

The winds and the waves kept up their tumult until after twelve o'clock, when to our great relief the ocean grew more tractable, and although we are sailing as fast, the motion is somewhat easier. The trade winds are blowing and we should make good progress. We are about 950 miles from the equator.

Wednesday June 16th. The sea is quieting down as if ashamed of its uproar. The weather is growing much warmer and as the wind blows off Africa, there seems a degree of sickliness in the atmosphere, far from being acceptable. I hope we have a quieter night.

Thursday June 17th. Fairly on our course. Three ships passed today. Flying fish again. Air soft and very warm. 12 degrees north of the equator. Commenced writing letters today.

Friday June 18th. This day has been remarkably hot; quite overpowering. We had a plentiful and heavy shower towards night, which somewhat refreshed us. I never saw it rain faster. Hurricanes and storms are a frequent occurrence in these waters. The Captain and mates watch the weather narrowly.

Mr. Waterson caught another bonito.

The Captain threw a bottle overboard today, containing a statement of our position—latitude and longitude—with the request that the finder would ascertain the "set" and the strength of the currents that had borne it to its place of capture. Bottles are not infrequently found to have floated some thousands of miles, borne on with a resistless tide. Annie could not forgo the opportunity of putting a "wishbone" and some similar wonders in with the paper to astonish the finder.

Saturday June 19th. Still very sultry—scarcely a breath of wind. Thermometer—80 degrees in the cabin .

This night witnessed the operation of "tacking ship." The Captain cried "Ready about." This was echoed through the ship and all hands were summoned. Each man seized his rope and waited further orders. Then the Captain sang out, "Put your helm down." Man at the wheel says, "Helm down." Then the Captain cries, "Hard a-lee." This was

The Helmsman –

echoed and immediately fore- and jib-sheets let go and fore-top-bowline. Captain cries, "Main topsail, haul." Round comes the mainsail, and mizzenyards fly round like a whirligig! At this moment all was excitement, even Rover racing with the men and feeling it his duty to "lend a hand." Captain then cries, "Force bowline, let go and haul," and then around comes the foreyard and here we are on the opposite tack, heading west by south.

Retired early, but the heat was so great we all went on deck again for an hour.

<u>Sunday June 20th.</u> A good breeze, but bearing us three points off our course; 6 degrees north of the line.

<u>Monday June 21st.</u> Sultry and oppressive. Two English vessels sailed very near us. How refreshing it is to see a ship, after gazing so long on naught but sea and sky—apart from the real grandeur of a ship in full sail on the open sea. Wind rising . . . the sea is becoming rougher.

<u>Tuesday June 22nd.</u> Hot; gentle breeze; smoother sea.

<u>Wednesday June 23rd.</u> Very warm without any wind. Mamma saw a beautiful nautilus today. She described it as resembling a lady's pink silk bag, with strings, as it floated by. The portion of it that appears above water is supported by a number of feelers underneath which act as rudders. When caught, if one happens to touch the nautilus, it stings very sharply. It belongs to the connecting link of fishes and marine vegetables.

<u>Sunday 27th June.</u> Some days have elapsed since I took any notes on account of the great heat and consequent lassitude. Today—33 days

from New York, longitude 25 degrees—at half past two in the afternoon, we "crossed the line" to our great satisfaction. We expected Neptune would have extorted a fee for crossing his path, as is his usual method, but for once the Captain maintained his dignity and no Neptune appeared. It has been a foolish custom in times past—more than now—that when a person crossed the equator for the first time, the sailors should shave him with an iron bar, or otherwise ill-treat him, unless he "stood treat" with money or ardent spirits. But, happily, this custom is being rapidly abolished, as it often was attended with pain and violent resistance.

Monday June 28th. Mr. East lost his cap overboard; a serious disaster, for we are in a situation where money will not purchase all one requires!

Wednesday June 30th. A fine day. The Captain called us to see more of the nautilus "Portuguese Man-O-War," as the sailors call them. They vary in size and color. Some bright pink and lavender, and some transparent. They somewhat resemble a child's miniature ship as they sail by on the tips of the waves. When anything impedes their progress, they are said to have the power of drawing in the delicate sail, which appears so attractive to the naturalist.

Today we have all guessed the day we land. Mr. East says October 17th; I, October 25th; Ma, November 1st; Annie, October 27th.

July 3rd. The last three days have been rough, the vessel has rocked and pitched very unpleasantly, making us all feel poorly again, but the wind favors us, and we are fourteen degrees south of the line, having made a thousand miles since Sunday. The weather is cooler. The moon has shone very brilliantly lately, and the Southern constellations are gradually making their appearance in full glory and in countless number. Moonlight at sea is always very beautiful—only at sea does the moon appear to perfection as it rises like a ball of fire from beneath the dark waters, "Queen of the Sea and Beauty of the Sky."

Sunday July 4th. This is the day that commemorates the Independence of America. The morning was very rough, the sea high, the vessel rocking tremendously. Had it not been for this, the Captain would have fired off our two cannon for a salute. Our consolation was that our vessel was on her course with a fair wind and we sailed about 10 knots an hour. We made a slight change in dress (as we have worn calico dresses all the time) in order to recognize the day as Sunday, and the Fourth, too. The Captain treated us to champagne. We also had a fine turkey and an astonishingly large plum pudding, that never-failing welcomer of all joyful occasions. After these articles, with their concomitants, were fully relished, we all felt contented and some of us partook of a refreshing siesta. The waves having "gone down," we all sat on deck until teatime, when occurred the greatest wonder of the day. Then, to the amazement of several of the party (ourselves excepted being in the secret) the steward inquired if some one would take a little milk! Snow in August would not have been more remarkable than a jug of milk at sea several thousand miles from land and without a cow. The Captain suggested poetically that the steward "must have milked the turkey," but we were informed previously that it proceeded from a packet of "congealed milk" given the steward by a friend in Portsmouth. And very palatable it proved to be, more than its appearance would have testified.

We went on deck after tea. Myriads of stars illumined the heavens, there being three or four times the number in the Southern Hemisphere than in the Northern, particularly those of the first magnitude. Never did I feel the full force of those beautiful lines of Addison's[4] so much as when gazing on this glorious "spangled sky" as Mr. East slowly repeated "The spacious firmament on high with all the blue ethereal sky." The moon rose about nine o'clock and came peeping out from the cover of a dark cloud as if modestly giving the stars notice they were about to be eclipsed. It needs no romantic ideas of love or poetry to lend enchantment to such scenes as these we have witnessed so far on our voyage of six weeks continuance.

<u>Monday July 5th.</u> Quite an excitement on board, owing to a brig "laying to" across our bow. We bore down on it, as Captain Jameson wished to confer on longitude, and so came very near. The Captains held quite a long conversation through their speaking trumpets over our position, but there was but little difference. Our visitor was the "Bessie" of Liverpool, whither she was bound from Callao [Peru]. Captain Jameson asked them to report us, the "Josephine."

Annie put an eyestone[5] in her eye to get out a lash, and fainted, came to, got the eyestone out, whereupon I threw it overboard to the discomfort of that lady and the displeasure of the company in general, but I wished to prevent a repetition of such a scene.

Tuesday July 6th. *Dear Papa's birthday—49 years old. Our ship glides along elegantly in full sail with a fine breeze aft; the most perfect sailing we have experienced. After the heat of the tropics and consequent prostration of strength, the exhilarating air is delicious. We expect to be opposite Rio [de] Janeiro soon.*

I have made up my mind not to say much about the passengers, so uncongenial are they to us in many ways, but there are some few individuals I must describe:

First our steward and stewardess: The latter is young, fat, and good-natured—no matter how the Captain swears (for I regret to say he is sadly addicted to this fearful habit) she preserves her equanimity, and to her, seasickness is only "an attachment." As for the steward, he is really a remarkable production of human nature; also young, active, somewhat below usual height, of pleasing countenance, he makes all pass smoothly. He possesses qualities far above his station, for not only can he produce delicacies to please the nicest appetite, or stoop to make your bed, or cheerfully perform any necessary business for your comfort and convenience, but at the same time, he will entertain you with some wild adventure he has experienced on whaling expeditions in the Pacific Ocean, or amid the beauties of Rio [de] Janeiro or Juan Fernandez.⁶

He is a literary steward too, having expressed as his opinion that no person is fit to mix in society who cannot recognize any passage in "Ivanhoe," setting aside all other works of thrilling interest, Shakespeare, etc. He is also the medical steward and can give advice regarding your health that would stagger some doctors.

That he is a cook, his well-served dishes may testify, and that he can wash and iron "first rate" his wife knows fully well, <u>which</u> person either does not possess any of these proficiencies, or else amiably considers her husband possesses enough for both.

Such then is our steward—a genius.

Our second mate too, Mr. Martin, is no less a character in his own way, though of a different style. Picture him, then, an older man, short, robust, and of ruddy complexion, and a particularly good-natured expression, being as he says, "no hand to meet trouble halfway." See him walking about in his shirtsleeves, ready for action and bearing about his carriage a "don't care" sort of air, that would do honor to a Pope or much less to a King. He wears his hat knowingly on one side, that to match it one must take lessons for one voyage at least, while from under its well-worn brim twinkle the smallest and merriest blue eyes ever placed in mortal man. But listen to him and I will engage, should Mr. Martin say it was rough—should he say in any way all was not well—I would not give much for our chances of reaching land, for never was there a more sanguine man. Go to him when you will, he tells you how well we are going, how much better we shall soon be, or how many impossible miles we have already gone.

Surely under a coarse exterior he carries a noble spirit that would cheer one in the darkest mood and drive the heaviest clouds away and almost rid one of seasickness, with his budget of good news.

July 7th. At last this Wednesday brings us a real stormy day—cold and wintry and dark. We all look grave again for our vessel plunges and rocks and shakes us as if neither wind nor water suited her. How changeful is our position! Surely "our sea is troubled."

July 8th and 9th, Thursday and Friday. Still dark and stormy. The ship sways distressingly over and over. Rolling, tumbling, slipping, sliding; everybody everywhere but where they would be! The weather ten degrees colder, too.

We have been delighted with the sight of the beautiful Cape pigeons, two of which have been captured by means of hooks baited with fat. They are very beautiful, varying in size from a wood-pigeon to a good-sized duck; their bodies covered with soft white-and-brown down. Their feet are webbed and their bills hooked. They fly at our stern, staying sometimes to rest on the turbulent waves as if on a smooth sea, sitting gracefully on the snowy crests, or diving far below the surface to seize some chance treasure thrown from our vessel. They cannot rise from the deck as they always run along the water before they fly and look so mild and dependent, it seems cruel to take them. When caught, they seem to have no fear of man, but were so sick (vomiting) when handled it was deemed expedient to send them back to their native element. No one knows where they breed or how they subsist, but they look very content as they waft about us.

July 10th and 11th, Saturday and Sunday. Two dark, stormy days. On Saturday night it blew a squall and a gale followed. We rolled about *at a great rate and felt, of course, very uncomfortable and disheartened. Sunday we suffered all day from the effects of the previous gale. The sea was so rough it seemed that our masts would certainly roll out of the ship and we had only the consolation of moving about 3 or 4 miles an hour. Our ship leaks about 10 inches an hour; three or four sailors are pumping every hour for a short time. This is a sorry prospect for us, with the worst of our journey to come.*

<u>July 12th, Monday.</u> No wind, almost a calm. Our beautiful companions, the pigeons, are still flying around us, defying all the angry winds and waves to drive them away. Nothing could move more gracefully than these lovely birds. Sometimes they sit on the water near the rudder and when a wave approaches you think would annihilate them, they gently rise on its bosom like the spray for very lightness. At other times, after flying in circles for some minutes, they will dive far below the surface in quest of food, and when you think they are gone, up they will come triumphantly with their booty.

We saw a whale today; it came up three times to blow and then all trace of it ceased. It was supposed to be a "right" whale, a species from which the greatest quantity of oil is produced. Mr. Waterson caught two pigeons, also an albatross with his bunch of hooks and pork bait. Its body was about the size of a common goose. When brought on deck it could neither fly nor walk, but it made a great show of attack on Rover, who retreated with still greater surprise. It had too formidable a bill to engage in even contact with him. It was found that with its wings out-

WRITTEN AT SEA, 1852

stretched it measured seven feet from tip to tip. Mr. Waterson killed it and cut the wings off and gave them to me to keep, but unfortunately they were in the way, so the steward threw them overboard.

July 13th, Tuesday. Mr. East's birthday. This is a mild, warm, calm day. We have been watching the Captain, expecting by the manner in which the vessel shapes her course, she is about to "put in" at *St. Catherines.* St. Catherines is a lively island off Brazil, a most desirable place to recruit our bodies and spirits for awhile and a place where we could obtain delicious fruits. Such a proceeding may detain us a fortnight. The ship leaks very much, but the Captain is unusually silent and mysterious; he keeps his own counsel at present.

It is rather trying to feel all our bright summer days are to be turned into cold winter hours round Cape Horn, the seasons being reversed in the Southern Hemisphere.

July 14th and 15th, Wednesday and Thursday. Our weather is mild and temperate; quite a pleasant change. Wednesday night one of our best sailors had the cholera. Mr. Gardiner, our first mate, gave him a plentiful dose of brandy and cayenne pepper, which restored him in a measure, but he looks extremely ill for so short an illness. About 10 o'clock a stillness reigned through the ship, but the practiced ear of the sailor detected shrill whistling in the distance and a small cloud could be seen making towards us. The sails were reefed and all made ready for a hurricane, which in a few minutes swept by us merely leaving a slight whirling sensation at our stern, felt only by the helmsman. So watchful *and careful is it necessary to be, a few moments inattention even to the clouds may endanger the ship. A man is kept near the bow of the vessel always on the lookout, while the Captain or one of the mates is always on the quarterdeck.*

July 16th, Friday. A dark, damp day. Off River de la Plata,[7] at which place we may expect bad weather. The mouth of this river is about 150 miles wide. These cold, raw days make us feel poorly. Mamma is not well from eating the potatoes, which at last are beginning to fail; they have been a great comfort to us so far. Captain threatened to "roast" the cook today, being a slight variation from his usual intention of licking him.

July 17th, Saturday. A brisk wind! Quite encouraging.

July 18th, Sunday. The first part of this never-to-be-forgotten day the wind was fair and we were making about 10 knots an hour. About four P.M. there was a lull and a pleasant evening seemed before us when suddenly the captain loudly hailed, "All hands," and soon, with a rising wind 19 or 20 men were seen hanging on the mainyard bracing the sail as fast as they could, which, from being wet and consequently very heavy, tested their united strength to the utmost. They had scarcely returned to the deck when the wind rose to an alarming height; orders were given and executed with astonishing rapidity, but the gale soon set in in good earnest and, Oh, what a gale! Never will it be effaced from my memory. The ship "lay to" under close reefed topsails; that is a nautical phrase implying she was made as fast and quiet as possible. The

wind actually roared like continuous thunder. Never have I heard a
sound so awful. The sea was lashed into fury, while wave after wave
dashed over us as if threatening instant destruction. It was indeed an
awful night. We did not undress, but sat silent and awestruck while with
almost breathless interest we listened to this war of the elements. Scenes
of happy hours spent with beloved ones on shore wafted o'er us while
ever and anon, as the fierce winds dashed about us, shaking our ship
from stem to stern, eternity seemed dawning near with all its fearful
results. We read of storms at sea, or shipwrecks and terrors of the deep,
but Oh, how little do we realize when by our fireside at home on dry
land, the horrors of being partakers of such scenes.

During this suspense a strange sound was heard, a rush and then a
cry of "Overboard!" Mercifully it was not as we thought, but it was some
minutes before we found the cause. The helmsman, one of our most
active and efficient sailors, an Italian, in endeavoring to hold the wheel
had been thrown over it, and it struck him three times before he was
relieved. It was thought at first his arm was broken, but happily for him
it was only badly bruised. As we have no physician, Mr. Waterson did
what he could for him, but he was in great agony for some time. Had he
gone overboard, no effort could have been made to save him, so violent
was the storm. About two o'clock it blew a hurricane; one of the sails
was torn to pieces.

<u>Monday, July 19th.</u> Last night I took two comforters or quilts and
made my bed on the floor for greater security. On arising this morning, I

*found one comforter saturated with salt water, the water having leaked
in through the second cabin and made us wet throughout. We had to put
on our India rubbers the first thing. The gale has somewhat abated but it
has left us with three cross-seas just as if one was not enough to break us
up. The Captain says he has no fear of Cape Horn if we get through this
storm without injury. Surely it seems like a fearful introduction to the
winter portion of our journey.*

*July 20th, Tuesday. Longitude 40. About the middle of last night the
gale ceased, our sails were raised, and we are once more sailing onward,
thankful that we are spared to enjoy rest—comparative rest—for the
time, from fatigue and terror.*

*July 21st, Wednesday. A calmer day, but cold and wet. Our Captain,
after considerable grumbling and shivering on the part of us passengers,
has at length put up our stove, and in spite of injury to the mahogany
veneering of the cabin, the gas and smoke of the fire, the extra risk of
being blown up and down too, and innumerable other inconveniences,
we welcomed that rusty little stove as an old friend with a cheerful countenance. It is laughable to listen to the variety of advice given ad libitum
by us passengers as to the best way of lighting the fire, and then the difficulties remain to be solved touching the keeping it in. The steward
tried again and again, but succeeded in producing only smoke. Finally
Mr. George Waterson came to the rescue and made a respectable fire,
which had a wonderfully cheering effect on us all. Indeed we have not
spent such a comfortable afternoon for some time. Whether our comfort*

is to be of long duration remains to be proved, as the Captain has raised among other objections to the stove that it is affecting the compass. Even Rover, who has moaned and groaned very much during the last rough weather, seems glad of the fire. A large ship is to be seen in the distance.

> The morning hours of cheerful light
> Of all the day is best
> But as they speed their hasty life
> If every hour is spent aright
> We sweetly sink to sleep at night
> And pleasant is our rest.
>
> But life is like a summer day
> It seems so quickly past
> Youth is the morning bright and gay
> And if 'tis spent in wholesome way
> We meet old age without delay
> And death is sweet at last.

Towards night our wind increased and once more a gale set in with redoubled fury; again we "lay to" and again the fierce wind returned to its roaring, and the sea to its boiling.

July 22nd, Thursday. The storm still continues, accompanied with squalls of sleet or hail nearly every half hour. We are nearly tired out. Our stove is a great comfort to us, being one in which we can see the fire. We sit around it on the floor holding fast to the fender. We have seen some strange scenes at the table, dishes with their contents upsetting in all directions.

July 23rd, Friday. The water has come in very much during the storm. The cabins are wet and miserable, and the poor sailors half drowned in the forecastle at the bow of the ship.

July 24th, Saturday. Our vessel is once again on her way after "laying to" 36 hours.

July 29th. The last five days have passed without any particular occurrence taking place. This day, Thursday, has been a very pleasant day, the best we have had for a fortnight, but we have made little progress. I have been able to draw a little. We have all been on deck too short a time; it seems like a Spring day on shore. What would we not give for a sight of land! We are somewhere near the Falkland Islands.

July 30th, Friday. Our vessel has glided along at the rate of 8 or 9 knots an hour with a fine breeze and as smoothly as if on a river, the very perfection of sailing. We expect to pass through the Straits of Le Maier tonight.

July 31st. After all, the Captain did not think it safe to go through the Straits, so we went outside which takes us many miles further; however, it is best to be careful. A dark morning, having light on our breakfast-table after 8 o'clock. It is rainy and cold. Our days last from 8 to 4 P.M. We are beginning to "double the Cape,"[8] which is by far the worst part of our journey and has hitherto been a terror to the most experienced seamen. It is indeed a dreary prospect for us; what would we not give if we were fairly round Cape Horn.

August 1st, Sunday. This day with its fearful results has been to us the

*most terrible of our passage. On entering the cabin this morning we found
the passengers around the stove and the snow was falling fast in large
flakes on deck. . . . What a contrast to any 1st of August we had seen
before! Soon after breakfast the sun broke out and the Captain took an
observation. We were very near the Cape and everything seemed dreary
and miserable indeed. During the day many things took place calculated
to distress and annoy us. [Lucy Kendall did not record what it was that distressed them so on this Sunday, but family tradition states that a sailor
carelessly went down with a lighted candle into the hold where the gunpowder was stored. Considering the combustible nature of the cargo,
nothing could have been more criminally negligent. On hearing it, the
Captain flew into one of his rages, and in a violent passion—which was
not entirely unwarranted—was about to have the man flogged. Only a
petition by all the passengers saved the man a beating.—Ed.]*

*Oh, how we longed for a Sunday where peace and order reigned and
where we could worship God in His Sanctuary. Yet we were better off
then than in that gale off the River de la Plata, for our vessel did not—
in the early part of the day—rock and labor as heavily.*

*We considered ourselves half way, and at 9 o'clock we were in our
beds thankful to finish a day that had been so painful to us. Oh, what an
awful night we were fast approaching! I had slept in the afternoon and
so, restless and wakeful, I listened anxiously to every sound on deck.
Presently, I heard the wind with its well-known roar approaching, and
with it came over me a feeling of such terror I had not felt before, and*

such as few can conceive sitting 'round a warm fire on a winter night on land. It seemed as though the scenes of the day, when passion had obtained unlimited sway in the person of the Captain, were about to be punished and in what way was too soon felt by all. . . . Yes, the gale had reached us, the wild waves dashed furiously by, to the noise of the hoarse wind, while at the rate of ten or twelve miles an hour we swept onward. The loud voice of the Captain was heard as he issued his stern orders to the poor shivering crew while eagerly they tore down the extra sails, when presently a strange noise, confused and troubled, was heard, and soon after I distinctly heard that one of our best, indeed <u>the</u> best, most able, active, and energetic seaman had—in reefing the jib-sail from the bowsprit—fallen overboard and was at that time struggling in the waves for life and yet no possible thing could be done to save him. . . . Boats we had in plenty but it was impossible to lower them into such a raging sea. Oh, how dreadful to feel we were leaving him to perish. . . . May I be spared such a scene again; to lie and fancy his vain struggles for deliverance, and then the pain of suffocation all coming under one's own immediate knowledge without the means of helping may be realized but not experienced.

We knew the man who was lost, well; we had seen him often at the helm—he was an Englishman but his parents were Irish, living in Dublin. One other man was thrown into the sea at the same time but a wave washed him up so that another old sailor caught him, but his back was seriously injured. At the time the poor fellows were sent out to reef that jib the bowsprit went 10 to 12 feet under water so one can form by this some idea how violently we were pitching. Only the best of the crew would attempt to do this, and the Captain was heard to say he would rather have lost three of the others than poor James McCann.

And this is the commencement of going round Cape Horn!

<u>Monday August 2nd.</u> A gloom is over us all; we feel that one of our number, young, handsome, and apparently the most hardy on board, has suffered a violent death and yet we are going on. The poor man's chest has been brought down the companionway and the Captain has taken possession of his clothes and papers. Among the latter was found a letter from his mother acknowledging the receipt of five pounds which he had sent her from his hard-earned wages. Oh, how that poor mother's heart will throb as she hears her son was drowned off Cape Horn. How will his brothers and sisters mourn for him who perished alone on the dark waters. As he was swept off the bowsprit he was heard to say, "My God, save me." He was a tall, powerful man about 25 years old. His clothes will be sold on board to his comrades and the amount of his wages will, I believe, be sent to his home. This is the customary thing for captains to do with the things belonging to those who perish at sea. This is the first man the Captain has ever lost overboard though he has been at sea 22 years and a long time captain.

<u>August 7th, Saturday.</u> This has been a trying week, cold, stormy, and dark. Eight hours light, sixteen hours night and still tossing about in the latitude of Cape Horn. The Captain wishes to make all the westing, or

rather longitude, he can before we go north. He does not mean to go into any port as we thought he would. We have 75 days' water now, and this he thinks will last; we still have poultry. Today we have had sunshine, squalls of snow, and flakes as we do not see often even in New York, and then sunshine followed or accompanied by hail. Strange weather; no dependence on it an hour.

Our steward has been ill, confined to his bed. Mr. Gardiner, the mate, has a bad hand. The poor fellow who hurt his arm is slowly recovering but he cannot use it yet, and the man who was rescued when the other was drowned has suffered dreadfully from inflammation in his back. Mamma made him some arrowroot in a contrivance she has of tin and an alcohol lamp, which comforted him, but any sailor is uncared for and neglected however ill, because he has no business to be sick! Oh, pity the wretched condition of the sick seaman, for truly there are few situations in life more perilous and distressing than that of the sailors. They are subject to the absolute authority of a man who—according to his humor—can promote or chastise. A slave has as little peace; and yet with a strange infatuation a sailor seems to cling to his vocation, though I believe in many cases it is more from sheer inability to earn his living in any other way than from any romantic affection for the treacherous ocean.[9]

I have seen and heard more on board this ship of a sailor's life and experienced more storms during this voyage than I ever should have imagined in crossing in one of the London packets; not but that we have every individual comfort we can reasonably expect, but the discipline is so severe that we live in constant fear of an outbreak. We shall not feel surprised at whatever quarter it bursts out first.

Three ships were in sight today. We have been on deck two or three times this week for a little while. Our stove is a great comfort to us. Mamma looks better and better indeed. We all keep well, have excellent appetites; all we require is the means of taking more exercise. Annie feeds her birds and wonderful to say they bid fair "to weather the Cape." No one need be afraid to take a voyage if he has once gone round this horrid Cape Horn. Many times, in the spirit of Dickens's Miss Jelleby do I say "the Cape's a beast."

Thursday, August 12th. I have not written since Saturday. Sunday we might say we had fairly doubled the Cape after being 8 days rounding it, which is considered a wonderful feat. Most ships are a longer time, some being six weeks in performing the same distance. We went down as far as 60 south, the longitude being 56 degrees. Cape of Good Hope is the same,[10] but Cape Horn is colder, and until the California emigration, few ships went round its stormy, barren coast. The inhabitants of this southern part of South America, the Patagonians, are very savage and barbarous indeed. None of the islands around here have been at all inviting and we had little to hope—even for our lives, had we been shipwrecked during the last month—from the natives on this coast.

Cape Horn is a rock jutting out into the sea and a strong wind from the land drives vessels away from the shore. The great difficulty is to keep near enough to round it, instead of being blown down to the extreme southern latitudes. I should like the Cape and its cold snows, storms, and "South Westers" to be blotted off the map and become annihilated on the earth. Never come to California round the Cape!

I went on deck one evening to see what are called the Magellan-clouds, named after the man who discovered the straits bearing the same name. They are black and white, the white resembling the milky way, while the black appear like blotches in the sky. They are always to be seen in these latitudes and some suppose them to be constellations of stars or heavenly bodies.

Monday and Tuesday we had a fine wind which has carried us far north west.

Wednesday. The Captain evidently means to "put in" at some port, either Valparaiso or Juan Fernando [Juan Fernandez] or Talcahuano.[11] He does not say, but his course is so directed. Our water is getting low and our chickens are beginning to feel lonely; if they could speak they would probably suggest that having weathered the Cape they ought to live in peace for the rest of their lives, especially as so many of their number have ministered to our necessities. Twelve only survive who, together with a few unhappy turkeys, lead a very restless and precarious life. Today we feel more and more thankful to think that more than half and by far the most dangerous part of our journey is over. We have been sailing very smoothly and pleasantly of late and Annie and I have been sewing at some shirts for dear Papa. We think of and talk over dear ones in England and America and of the beloved Papa we are getting nearer and nearer, until our brains ache from anticipation for the result of this great undertaking.

We do not yet know the Captain's intentions but we are going north east, which of course proves we shall soon be near land. Our latitude is about 46 and our longitude near 80. How many thousands of miles we have travelled! Our path is so circuitous, so controlled by the winds we scarcely ever sail in a direct course for many hours together.

Our fellow-passengers are very little company, being three illiterate mechanics and Mrs. Waring, who is a wicked, vulgar, mischief-making, ugly old maid (although married about six years). She is five-feet, eight inches high, as thin as a lath, with no teeth but an occasional false set which, when she wishes to laugh, puts in for the purpose. I would not speak thus, but we have never before been in such low and barbarous society, and at sea, unfortunately, there is no alternative but to bear it. Mr. East rarely makes any comment on the movement of parties around him derogatory to their walk and conversation, but he has solemnly asserted that Mrs. Waring is not by any means a proper person to associate with and, in a general way, we barely exchange common civilities. It would greatly add to our comfort and thereby diminish the tediousness of the voyage had our fellow passengers been more companionable, but we content ourselves under existing conditions with the possibilities of there being no reason for complaint in other respects.

Friday, August 13th. Another unpleasant day. We had a head wind and from its results on the Captain's temper we have learnt to dread its existence as much as a severe gale. Just at one o'clock, our dinner hour, the steward privately informed the Captain that our soup was burnt, and the Captain being in no humor to be trifled with and having, as he said, a blacklist against the cook which was always threatening to pay off—in a violent passion by way of keeping his threat—and being revenged on the wind at the same time—straightway dashed to the galley where he caused the poor old man to be tied by his hands to the rigging, and after summoning the sailors and boys as witnesses, beat him with a knotted rope.

It was not the Captain's intention that we ladies should know what was going on but ill news always travels very fast, and I question if in reality the subject of this piece of monstrosity suffered more than we did. Such a heartsickening and loathing sensation overwhelmed us, it seemed as though we were accessory to a foul murder, and yet so complete is the authority of the Captain no one passenger or servant dare move a foot to prevent the disciplining of the ship on pain of confinement, if not irons. Whatever may be the transgression, however unjust the punishment, there is no redress except at the end of the voyage. In the present instance we were relieved to find the cook had not been hurt much, but the mortification had been severe and the law forbids flogging, so the Captain will be summoned when we arrive at San Francisco.

The stewardess told me that the cook had the rope with which he was whipped and was going to lock it in his chest. What a terror it has cast over us; indeed of late, head winds, accidents, loss of life, violent scoldings, swearings, and now this flogging have cast such a gloom and *depression over us I feel we are really in a very unenviable position.*

Mr. Waterson caught a large albatross, of a gray color, nearly as large as a swan and measuring between nine and ten feet across the body and wings. It has a long pink bill.

<u>Saturday, August 14th.</u> Still uneasy and longing to be away from this scene of discord. No one can realize the misery of being among comparative strangers on a wild and raging ocean; thousands of miles away from home with a swearing, impetuous Captain and a consequent unhappy, dissatisfied crew; feeling every change of wind will cause a fresh outbreak, in perhaps the only quiet corner of the ship. Oh, for dry land where, though the wind whistles mournfully through the tall trees and the snow and rain beat against the windows, one can draw near their cheerful fire made ten times brighter by the company of dear ones around, and pity the poor traveler on his perilous voyage.

Very little poetry is there in a sailor's life. With very few clothes and as much tobacco as he can scrape together, he sets out to sea, and months after he is spoken of as having been a wild restless spirit, though a good-natured fellow, and it was the best thing he could do. See him, then, as he journeys on to take his place in the forecastle—to which an Irish hovel is preferable! At the bow of the vessel it ships the fiercest head seas or possibly—as in this ship—the vessel leaks. Then be sure the sailor suffers most; his clothes (the few he has though it is winter) become saturated, his coarse mattress soaked through, nothing but perhaps a wet blanket on him, he lies down to rest (if rest it may be called).

Restlessly he rolls on his wretched bed; at length, worn out, he falls asleep. Oh happy moment, the only one the sailor dares to have, when he may dream of home and bright scenes and faces far away. He dreams on and the joys of happy days are within his grasp when now a savage voice awakens him and a rude grasp seizing him warns him to his post. Aching and racked with pain in the dark stormy night, he is ordered aloft to reef the highest sails. When unable to resist the violence of the wind and elements and giddy from his unfinished slumber, his grasp relaxes, a wild wave receives him, one cry, a splash, "Man overboard" is shouted but alas! he is gone! A frequent occurrence, but who remembered the poor sailor? His mother may think of her child at sea but she only fancies him doing the work of that fine ship she saw in the dock, sailing smoothly on the great sea. Who will tell her, if they know, that he will not more return to the home of his childhood? Oh pity the sailors, they suffer more than tongue can tell aboard these merchantmen!

The Captain took down the evidence of some of the witnesses tonight. He will surely not escape unscathed some day.

<u>Monday, August 16th.</u> Longitude 42. We are going to anchor at some port soon. A pipe, which was oiled, was suffered to fall into the tank that contains our drinking water, and now we are almost sick with the taste. I hope we shall be able to get fresh provisions to last to the end of the voyage; hitherto the table has been well furnished, but our good things are waxing scarce.

<u>Tuesday, August 17th.</u> Last night both Mamma and I were awake

most of the night. It blew a gale and indeed roaring is the only description of the tone of wind in a gale at sea; we never hear the same sound on land. It is very awful and doleful—as if threatening the ship with inevitable destruction—and tons of water broke over the vessel, enough to make the stoutest heart shudder. The waters of the Pacific had been so tranquil compared to those of the Atlantic, we hoped the gales were over. However, we do not bat about below quite as much as in former storms. Oh, how we long to be on land at home once more! I feel no inducement could tempt me to sail on a long voyage again.

The birds, albatross and Cape pigeons, still follow us by hundreds, the former being much larger than ever. The Captain said he saw one today that measured 14 feet.

This has been a very rainy day with unfavorable winds. All seems discontent and general dissatisfaction.

<u>Wednesday, August 18th.</u> We were awake last night about 12 o'clock when it was blowing hard on deck and we could hear the sailors tacking ship with all their strength. Today we find that at that time we were within ten miles of land and had it not been for the great watchfulness of the Captain (which seems to be his only redeeming quality) we should assuredly have gone on until perhaps too late to remedy our condition, for the night was dark and the mate did not see the land.

We have a full view this morning of the mountains on the Isle of Mocha, about 25 miles off the coast of Chile [and about 275 miles south of Valparaiso—Ed.]. This island is not inhabited; we are about twenty miles *distant but as some portions of the range of mountains are 1,300 feet above the level of the sea, I have been able to take a rough sketch of them.*

This is the first land we have seen for 85 days and yet it brings little pleasure—we are experiencing such changeable weather. Now sunshine and then a hail-squall, and then a sea in a great tumult throws us about violently.

Millions of the little fish called sardines are playing round the ship last night and between the squalls the stars shone with unusual brilliancy and appeared twice their ordinary size.

Thursday, August 19th. A fair wind and making our course towards land. From all we can glean we now suppose our destination is Talcahuano. Rather disappointed—Valparaiso being a much pleasanter place. Talcahuano was visited by a very terrible earthquake and tidal wave some years since, which very nearly destroyed the town. Mamma and Annie are on deck, the sun shining and the air soft and pleasant but it will take a good long time on land before I recover from the effects of terror and anxiety which for six weeks past have been our portion.

Friday, August 20th. We came very near the land.

Saturday, August 21st. We came in full view of the mountains of Chile, but owing to the rugged coast, we slipped by Talcahuano before the Captain was aware of it, very much

Annie hoisting sail.

92

to the delight of most of us as we all preferred seeing Valparaiso. The mountains are very high; first appears the cliff, then above long ranges of hills and still higher, towering far in the clouds, soar the icy mountains [The Cordilleras[12]] which branch from the Andes. It would be a vain attempt to portray the feelings of delight and admiration which filled our minds while gazing on this all-imposing scene.

Sunday, August 22nd. A beautiful sky, land in full view. The first object, after seeing the telegraph station which was placed on a prominent point, was the Barracks, and so near did we sail we could easily discern persons on horseback galloping gaily over the slopes and even the dresses they wore. This was a cheering sight after gazing on the same faces without any change for 89 long days. Gradually we approached a ridge of rocks jutting far into the sea, and all at once our vessel turned round it. A few minutes more and we were sailing into the harbor of Valparaiso, one of the wildest and most picturesque cities in the world, if such indeed it may be called, composed of a few Roman Catholic churches and a number of low built houses, as it lies on the border of the ocean. At the base of the mountains and scattered in all the crevices of the hills it appears as though the houses had fallen from the clouds and rolled down the hills, settling anywhere indiscriminately. At last we let fall the anchor close by an American frigate, the "Rariton."[13] Many ships lay close to us and boats approached from various directions. The rope ladder was put over the side when the Captain of the Port boarded us to see the ship's papers.

As he appeared above the gangway his hat blew off and Rover made advances in rather too warm terms to be pleasant—suggesting a hasty retreat to that august individual; but he eventually descended into the cabin followed by a Chilean servant, the first we had seen closely. Two of these Chileans came on deck; well-formed but heavy-looking, they struck us as being quite different to any human beings we had seen before. They wore scarlet scarfs round their waists instead of braces to their trousers, and a very white shirt and a small wind cap completed their costumes.

I was sitting in the cabin when a gentlemen entered, bowed to me, and in the true style of Dickens's Jingle gave me a hasty sketch of the city, its inhabitants, climate, earthquakes, and languages. So communicative was he, opening a Spanish Bible and proceeding to give me the sound of the different letters and words in such a continuous strain of eloquence, that it hardly seemed possible that he could be of sound mind. However, I found out that he was an American, had resided in Valparaiso two years, married a Chilean, and was a ship's chandler; which last piece of information had I known it at first, would have in some measure have accounted for his ardor and nobility in all that concerned the ship! His name is Potter and the firm to which he belongs is one of the best in this strange city. If you ever go to Valparaiso, I hope you will meet with this compound of Yankee acuteness and activity.

The Captain and gentlemen went on shore. We decided to wait till the morrow—it being Sunday—and we were well satisfied. The scene was very beautiful and in the evening, after the 8 o'clock gun had been *fired, we were entertained with music from the frigate's band. Although we regretted it was of a secular kind, added to the wildness of our situation and the stillness which it alone broke, the effect was delightful.*

August 22nd, Monday. We are pleased to find we have been very fortunate in our voyage compared to the other ships just arrived from the Cape.

We dressed ourselves early for the landing. The Captain, attended by the indefatigable Potter, came on board and as we had no chair to be hoisted over the ship's side, our only alternative was to go down the rope ladder. Here again Mr. Potter showed unusual alacrity; seizing the ropes, he mounted the gangway and commissioning us each (for he took us all down) to hold tight and step slowly, in the course of ten minutes we were all seated in the boat gazing up at the strange prison we were leaving for the first time in three months. Even Mrs. Waring was with us, under the especial protection of Mr. Cole.

As we ascended the steps of the quay, we were struck with the foreign appearance of everything around. Many Chileans were lounging about the square, wearing ponchos, or small square blankets of various patterns with a hole in the center to slip their heads through, then suffered to fall carelessly over their shoulders. They stared with great indifference at us. Our attention was directed to a Chilean attired as the rest, wearing the blanket in lieu of a coat, and mounted on a donkey while in stately grandeur he led two other donkeys laden with what appeared to be his wares. He slowly pursued his way and had it been to the grave, he could not have been more solemn.

The vehicles struck us as being very unsightly, very much resembling a doctor's shabby cab, to which were harnessed two horses, one being so much on the side it seemed to be more for ornament than use had it not been that the driver always rode on it postillion fashion.

Then came the ladies: short in stature, swarthy complexions, coarse features, low foreheads, jet-black hair and eyes, and round heads. They wore no bonnets, but over untidy dresses (beneath the hems of which might be seen what was once a white slip now dragging along dusty pavements) was thrown a shawl which, with some, was placed on the head and as it fell one corner was gracefully folded on the left shoulder. This struck me as being stylish, but notwithstanding the silk dress, the rich shawl, and occasional black veil worn on the back of the head, there was so much evident negligence and slovenliness about their general appearance we were not at all prepossessed in favor of them.

The streets are narrow, while two persons only can walk abreast on the pavement. Almost everything is imported; we tried in vain to find anything either useful or ornamental of native manufacture. French, English, and Americans are very numerous and conduct most of the business of the place. The Spanish language is generally understood, while the Chilean is a compound of Portugese, French, and Spanish.

We walked up and down the principal street, running parallel to the sea. The houses are mostly of one story in height, scarcely any windows, the doors being large enough to admit light and air, and at the same time giving the passerby an opportunity of surveying the domestic arrangements of the family, together with the furniture, etc. But this refers to the common Chilean dwellings, while in some parts of the city you may meet with a well-built house said to be magnificently furnished, but owing to the frequency of earthquakes which occur almost monthly, and the effect of volcanoes which abound in the interior of Chile, no substantial dwellings are erected. The city is one mass of dilapidated buildings, dirty, dusty rough streets, and lazy idlers or clumsy natives.

We went into a French restaurant and partook of some cake and chocolate, a fine treat. We also bought some dresses at a French draper's. Sometimes we would ask a question of a storekeeper and he would shake his head, not understanding us. Mr. East wished to purchase a cap to take the place of the one he lost overboard. We saw a native store and tried the door; it was locked. We were turning away when the owner, who stood some distance down the street, espied us; quickly he motioned for us to wait and started off like a shot. We were tired of standing when back he came with a key and two interpreters. We went in but he had not an article worth wearing in the cap line, and you may imagine how vexatious we felt after waiting so long and three gentlemen to attend us and nothing to deal with!

We went to Mr. Potter's store, where we found that gentleman and the Captain. Our letters were given to the English Consul, although we first visited the American Consul. We then purchased a bottle of raspberry vinegar. While doing so a short, sallow little gentleman approached us, and shaking hands all round, informed us his name was Fisher. He was

Chaplain of the American frigate and, after holding a few minutes conversation, he bowed himself off. We afterwards discovered he was a Greek.

Annie wishing to obtain some green stuff for her canaries, we turned up what appeared to be a narrow street in order to gain the hills. Our progress was slightly impeded by the donkeys which emerge from every point, herding by fifties on the beach, and—suddenly appearing in all possible places—strike you as being the principal inhabitants of Valparaiso. Indeed the poor specimens of horseflesh we met with seemed to be strangely out of place, while the donkey seemed to be exactly in his own sphere.

Up this rugged, dirty, steep, circuitous road we climbed; on each side of us were wretched-looking hovels with dirty old women and still dirtier children at the doorways. Most of them seemed to be cooking over a little fire in a furnace a concoction of green corn and molasses, while others might be seen seated inside on the floor eating something equally nauseous. Never shall I forget the savage and barbarous state of things in this, the chief city of Chile. At length finding neither green leaves nor a pleasant pathway, we gradually began to descend, now and then taking a look at the heterogeneous mass of homes below and around us. At length we found ourselves once more in Mr. Potter's store, after having scoured the neighborhood for fruit and finding nothing but apples, oranges, and figs—it being the last month of winter at Valparaiso.

There we found the Captain who told us he had one of Kossuth's lieutenants going out with us to San Francisco. We took a seat in the store,

98

where we were greatly amused at the variety of men, their costumes and language, which were transacting business around us. Captains, merchants, sailors, speculators, officers, and private individuals, all seemed engrossed in their separate interests.

I had almost forgotten to mention that one of our first steps was to find the post office at which place, after looking over the list, we were delighted to find a letter from Papa. This gave us fresh spirits, but having seen and obtained all that was possible we were only waiting to rejoin our ship. Mr. Martin was waiting for us; the Captain helped us into the boat, and by teatime we were once more on board. Having spent a delightful but fatiguing day, we were quite glad to get home and still more so that we were not obliged to live in the city of Valparaiso!

<u>Tuesday, August 23rd.</u> About the middle of the morning, the boat was lowered and the gentlemen, Annie, and myself, under the guidance and protection of Mr. Martin, set forth to board the American frigate. Not having seen a man-of-war, this promised to be a treat. We obtained immediate permission to board the frigate. On reaching the deck, the Captain came out of his cabin, welcomed us on board, took us into his room, apologized for its not being in perfect order, and after offering us some sherry, he, with the First Lieutenant and followed by other gentlemen, escorted us about the ship. We first went down on the gun-deck and then into the armory. This last place was very interesting, the arms brightly polished in their racks; several Indian war implements, paintings, drawings, and curiosities were found here. Still lower, we came to the deck

where the sailors hung their hammocks and took their meals and, passing by this, a small room where the midshipmen were enjoying themselves with a violin and an approaching dinner. We came into the ward room; here we met with the surgeons and in this room the lieutenant and surgeons, take their meals. We were regaled with champagne, apples, and oranges, all sitting around the table and treated as invited guests.

The Captain (Captain Dale) informed me of many interesting things; one of which is the possibility of their being called to go to Acapulco as the Mexicans had been ill-treating the Americans there.[14] The "Rariton" was out on a three-year cruise; two had passed, and one year more would elapse before that number of men—460—would see their homes.

Captain Dale was quite a venerable-looking gentleman; he spoke of home feelingly and also told me he had a child 18 months old he had never yet seen. The Fleet Lieutenant showed us his bedroom, which was quite a little sanctum. After staying quite a long time, the gentlemen not seeming disposed to return to the "Josephine," and I, inwardly fearing that Captain Jameson would return and wish to put out to sea, suggested a move, and soon after we bade adieu to the frigate. We had been greatly gratified with the sight and even more at the extreme cordiality and politeness we had received from perfect strangers. Americans are always polite to ladies.

On our return we were quite merry, particularly Mr. Martin, who, though not one of the cabin party, still expressed himself in glowing terms declaring that "he knew we should be well treated or he would not have wanted us to go."

On reaching the vessel we found that a new passenger was going with us—a Hungarian refugee. I need not say with what real pleasure I found this. I will now try and describe him. He is of noble family, an intimate friend of Kossuth's and Bereney's, and has fought in the late struggle. He is perfectly wild in his enthusiasm for Kossuth and seems to love him dearly. In person he is of the medium height, a fine large head, dark hair and an immense mustache, rather dark complexion, high forehead, and large intelligent eyes. Indeed he is a perfect gentleman by birth and education. Manners soft and gentle as a woman, he looks a very giant for strength. His conversation is intellectual, winning, and highly entertaining. He gains on your sympathy and affection at once; I never saw such a noble countenance.

We have now been at sea over a week. We sailed the next day with a fair wind—the 25th of August—aided by Mr. Potter, who, first to meet, was last to see us off. While the sailors drew up the anchor he stood by the helm, and as he vigorously turned the wheel he accompanied the evolutions with frantic gesticulations to the native boatmen who were around us, and some such phrases as these: "Who says we have no wind in Valparaiso?" "Who says there are no snakes in Virginia?" and other poetic remarks.

At length we were all ready—"Goodbye to all separately"—said Mr. Potter and over the vessel he flew, jumped into the boat almost losing his balance, caught the helmstrings—still standing at the risk of a cold bath, bowing to us, as the wind took his coattails and raving to his boatmen—so *appeared this singular man as he scudded back towards Valparaiso.*

Farewell thou city of mountains and volcanoes and earthquakes; pleasant has been our visit but may we never see thee more!

<u>*September 5th.*</u> *I have omitted several days in this my journal, for the first part of the time after sailing I was very sick, and owing to the change to fresh fruit and vegetables, I felt like commencing a fresh voyage. We have plenty of fowls, water, apples, oranges, eggs, cabbages, onions, pumpkins, and potatoes. The Captain has been in excellent spirits for the winds have been favorable; our latitude is about 21.*

Mr. Weisberger, which is only an assumed name for our new and noble fellow-passenger, is the greatest acquisition we could wish, full of anecdotes and incidents connected with travel over most parts of the world. He amused us for hours; he speaks English well, is able to talk in five or six languages, fond of music, drawing, and every refined pursuit; generous, unsuspicious, and open himself, he sheds a brightness round our way and our voyage has a pleasanter coloring than before.

Mr. W. neither drinks, smokes, chews, swears, nor anything objectionable. Remarkably dignified in person and manner, he forbids familiarity, and yet so contained and polite you feel easy at once in his presence. The other men seem to view him with envy, in reality caused by a sense of inferiority, the contrast being so great that words cannot describe. We are well acquainted now, and many nice chats we have. I do not know if he is really religious, but he possesses qualities that would grace a Christian. He was one of the four colonels or gentlemen of Kossuth's

suite who rode before him on his entrance to New York. He plays dominoes with us all, and having a very merry laugh, we feel quite cheered
up and as if we were in civilized society again.

Oh that we were at the end of our voyage! Valparaiso has shortened it
and Mr. W. has added to our comfort, but once more on terra firma may
we never set sail again!

Thursday, September 9th. Since I wrote last Saturday we have had
some of the best sailing we have experienced during our voyage.

Monday, September 13th. We have had fifteen days delightful sailing
during which time we have seen great numbers of whales, dolphins, flying fish, and a singular sort of bird called a gowney.[15] Our latitude is
about 3 degrees south of the equator, longitude 103, and we hope in
about thirty days to reach San Francisco.

Since the first few days of our leaving Valparaiso we have not seen
any ships. I ventured to assert that we should probably be at the equator
by Sunday. Yesterday the Captain and I had a wager on it; of course I
lost, it was a cigar, and today I gave him a little case holding the cigar
which he has promised to keep. We are full of anticipation as our voyage
promises to draw near a close. The weather is too warm to make work-
ing a pleasant occupation and our books are well-nigh exhausted. We are
again more inclined to sit on deck than set about any occupation below.
The stars shine forth with unlimited brilliance and the milky way is
brighter than ever.

One thing we have remarked as being a proof that the moon has *great influence on the water: we have never experienced bad weather when the moon has been at the full, but our worst storms have occurred on the darkest night.*

I persuaded the Captain to read "Pickwick" today. Annie and Mr. Weisberger have long discussions on various subjects. We like this gentleman very much, but he is occasionally so reserved and dignified, it is rather hard to make him out. He must certainly find it difficult to find means to render himself at ease with persons so unlike himself in station and education. Mrs. Waring has taken her place among the officers and servants of the ship, only appearing at mealtimes.

Our new Valparaiso dresses are finished. During their progress Mr. Weisberger seemed very much interested, and his remarks caused us no little amusement.

<u>Tuesday, September 14th.</u> Within about two degrees of the line—very warm, thermometer 78. Had conversation with Mr. Weisberger respecting Hungary, its nobility, peasantry, houses, and customs. It is very instructive and amusing to listen to his tales, garnished with the enthusiasm and feeling characteristic of the Hungarian. This afternoon finished two drawings of Valparaiso—on deck aided by the Captain in drawing a ship. Saw hundreds and hundreds of flying fish; the water seemed to be alive with them. We sail rather slowly today, but the last few weeks have been by far the most delightful of our voyage. Mr. Weisberger showed me some poetry he very much admired, one of Elize Cook's "Nature's Gentleman"—as follows:

Nature's Gentleman

Whom shall we dub gentleman:—The knave, the fool, the brute,—
If they but own full tithe of gold and wear a courtly suit;
The parchment scroll of titled line, the riband at the knee,
Can still suffice to ratify and grant such high degree:
But Nature with a matchless hand, sends forth her nobly born,
And laughs the paltry attributes of wealth and rank to scorn;
She molds with care a spirit rare, half human, half divine;
And cries exulting, "Who can make a gentleman like mine?"

Another, headed "A Character" was, as he termed it, the best piece in the book.

<u>Wednesday, 15th.</u> Crossed the line about 8 o'clock at night. Longitude 107.

<u>Thursday.</u> Had the last turkey but one for dinner on the occasion of crossing the equator.

<u>Friday, September 17th.</u> The weather has been very warm but we have had a gentle favorable breeze that has made us sail smoothly and pleasantly, sometimes without the slightest motion. I have nearly completed a picture of Langford.

This afternoon I went on deck intending to read, but Mr. Weisberger, declaring I had complained of weak eyes, took my book out of my hands and marched downstairs with it. Returning soon after, we became engaged with a game of dominoes, and while playing he told me of his friend, Col. Bereney, and of his own name, Maurice, also much of interest connected with Hungary, Kossuth, and his amiable wife. He is much above our sphere, but still he is so mild and gentlemanly we cannot but like his company.

Saturday, September 18th. We are now about a degree and a half north of the line. It has been a very, very warm day—80 degrees, 84 outside. We wander about scarcely knowing how to employ our time, being almost too warm to think—much more to work. I have been sketching part of the time—talking to, or rather listening to, Mr. Weisberger.

A fine ship has been in sight all day, but we cannot tell the name of it, and between etiquette and policy neither of the Captains is willing to draw nearer. Still, it is refreshing to see a sail and this is a very large, handsome ship. It is about three weeks since we have seen a vessel. The fish on this side, whales, porpoises, flying fish, and bonito are extremely numerous. We have a favorable light breeze and appreciate it all the more as we expected only calms and light winds in these latitudes. We, who have been so long together will soon part, but we have not, I think, any feeling of regret.

Sunday September 19th. This has been a very warm day. The Captain gave me a parcel of tracts[16] which were very acceptable; but we all felt overpowered, Mr. John Waterson particularly. Indeed, he exhibited some very striking symptoms of insanity; he had been exposed to the sun, and its effects in these latitudes are very bad. One of the men is ill from the extreme power of it during his midday watch at the wheel. Mr. Weisberger feels the heat exceedingly.

Our fellow traveler is in sight, but being a lighter ship she gains on us a little.

Monday September 20th. Warmer than ever—thermometer 84 in the shade and up to 120 on deck. We scarcely know what to do; I have tried drawing and reading, lying down and sitting up, the cabin and deck, all in vain—nothing is left but to submit. Our vessel moves slowly along. Everyone looks unpleasantly hot and shiny. Our fans are a great requisition. Mr. Weisberger is a great comfort in every sense of the word, always having something amusing at hand either to say or do.

Tuesday September 21. Annie's birthday, 16 years old, and we are 17 weeks out today. Mr. Weisberger gave her a bottle of perfume for her birthday—it is a very hot one.

Wednesday and Thursday, September 22 and 23. The thermometer is 80 degrees in the morning in the cabin. How we long for a cool breeze— instead of which we have a head wind! Many fish—large black fish, dolphins, flying fish—are every now and then playing round our vessel. A head wind always affects the Captain's health and temper to such a degree I dread it as much as a gale; he is more mad than sane on such occasions. We are in latitude 10 degrees.

Thursday a dark cloud rose called a Panama squall—for here we expect squalls—and the rain fell in showers. The wind soon raised the sea; the ship was tacked twice in less than an hour. We have been sailing so delightfully the last month with scarcely any motion and a prosperous wind that we are quite spoilt. The heat and head winds of the last few days are very discouraging to us. The squall brought us a fair wind that carried us along 9 or 10 knots, but after the rain ceased the wind changed again and, notwithstanding all the swearing and impetuosity of the Captain, gained the ascendancy and we are now, Friday the 24th, creeping south west with all the heat and consequent prostration of the previous time.

I have enjoyed my drawing very much—work is out of the question. I tried it this morning but was soon obliged to relinquish it. Various are the surmises respecting our arrival at San Francisco; a fair wind comes we shall be there in ten days, a head wind, one, two or more months. Uncertain, changeful, and desponding, we are ever complaining; but how much better are we off than many traveling the same road. We are in good health to begin with, and who can too fully appreciate this blessing? Another consideration, in a different light—yet to me scarcely more delighted in, is the fact of there being no children on board to cry and pine and make us feel worst of all. I suppose this would be called a negative mercy.

Annie and Mr. Weisberger have many long chats. I am always pleased to listen to her when arguing with him, for he calls in question much she says in order to make her express more fully her opinions. She certainly expresses herself very clearly and chooses suitable and choice words to set forth her ideas.

We all like Rover very much; strange to say, being a Newfoundland dog he is the most even-tempered creature on board, and certain it is his temper is the most tried. He may do a thing with a fair wind that will bring down vengeance on his head in a contrary one.

We spend a great deal of time on the transom close by the stern windows, but we seek in vain for any cool, refreshing air.

Tuesday 28th. The weather has continued very hot and oppressive. We have not known where to go or what position to assume to get cool and comfortable, the thermometer being 80 degrees in the morning and going two or three degrees higher towards the middle of the day.

A fine large ship has been in sight all day. We have now very singular birds flying around us—mostly white and gray, larger than a common pigeon and having one feather in their tail.[17] As they pass over, with their wide wings and stretched-out necks, they have a singular appearance. Mr. East captured a pretty little bird that flew on board for rest; its companion remained on the wing. It was between a sparrow and a martin and although not web-footed, and evidently a land bird, it would not eat and Annie, to whom it had been given, brought it on deck and it soon rejoined its mate and continued hovering round us for some time.

A large stupid bird called a booby[18] came on deck a short time since; none of these sea birds can fly off the ship; when once caught they are at the mercy of their captors.

Annie has had a large—or rather important—addition to her collection of marine insects in a small miniature fish, in shape resembling a shark, glittering like silver, and about the size of a small bean—it is very beautiful.

Wednesday September 29th. Last night was another eventful one. Five weeks ago we left Valparaiso, and our course has been smooth and pleasant, notwithstanding the head winds, that we were ill prepared for a violent thunderstorm which had been gathering all the previous afternoon. It lasted from 11 o'clock until half past one—just the dead of night, and very fearful it was. The lightning vivid, and loud continuous thunder, and the rain fell in torrents. Never had we heard it rain so before; indeed, sometimes such volumes of water fell it seemed as though we should be pressed down and founder. Dear Mamma was very much terrified. We both arose and partially dressed ourselves; the gunpowder on board did not diminish our terror.

This morning our companion of the previous day (the ship) came after us, bounding along like a bird. Although the rain continued falling unceasingly, we all went on deck and were repaid for the effort, for never had we seen a prettier spectacle. The ships were both sailing fast but our pursuer gained on us, rapidly slipping down on us with gracefulness. Presently she reached us and, bounding within a few yards of our lee-side, the ships drew in their forces—and then came the trumpets! Both vessels had all the passengers and crew on deck and we could see women and children on board our friend, but what could exceed the astonishment of the party when on asking the name of the vessel their Captain shouted "The 'Witch of the Wave,' 99 days out." It was none other than the allowed fastest ship in the world, and Captain Jameson was not a little proud of his conqueror.

Captain Jay of the "Witch,"[19] in accordance with Captain Jameson's wishes, then sent a boat with the first mate and a passenger to us to get some potatoes; they not having put in anywhere were out of these luxuries. While the mate was settling the matter in the Captain's room we had full benefit of the passenger's company. It was a laughable, though to us, extremely interesting sight, that of a visit here in the middle of the Pacific.

The passenger was a short, stout little man, very communicative, very important, and very much inclined to laud all connected with his own ship. He had sailed a month after us and so it may readily be conceived how he was interrogated. To all inquiries he replied as a matter of course, and as he stood in the middle of us, one might have guessed he was some natural curiosity just dropped from the clouds. He was, I am sure, a character, and could we have studied him longer, perhaps worthy of analyzing. As it was, we gleaned all the information we could in about ten minutes, and—having each of us written a few words to Papa, as it was acknowledged the ship would arrive some days before us—we bid adieu then and there. I was certainly glad when the "Witch" had the little man and his party safely back again.

And now as we started again, a nice little breeze came up. At first we left the "Witch" a little astern and we had as many sails hoisted as we dare carry, but in vain; no sooner did that "Witch" recover herself a little than on she came, and, as if gaining strength by the delay, overtook us, sailing gloriously by, settling like a swan on the waves, and soon after was to us as a passing dream whose influence was felt but not accountable.

We have seen and "spoken many ships" but this was by far the most beautiful sight we have had. For some hours we sailed very fast but our vessel, though a good sailor, is heavily laden and not as sharply built as a regular clipper. We are furnished for a fresh topic for discourse during this day.

October 3rd, Sunday. The heat has continued great and our adverse winds have prevailed nearly ever since we left the line. Our latitude is 18, longitude 122. We have sailed west instead of north west. Our wind today has veered favorable, and the trade winds so anxiously looked for have at length arrived, we think. Trade winds are those winds which during certain seasons in certain latitudes blow steadily from one quarter and of course are favorable to commerce and are depended on by all seafaring men. Now we are hoping to be in San Francisco in ten days or a fortnight.

October 4th, Monday. Mamma's birthday. Our fair wind continues; we are sailing along fast. We saw a large school of porpoises this morning—they leaped quite out of the water. It was a fine sight. We were going too fast to catch any.

Tuesday October 5th. We are traveling along at a good rate and are less than a thousand miles from San Francisco. Our countenances are quite brightening up, and yet with what strange and varied emotions do we each regard the future!

October 6th, Wednesday. Our fine wind died away in the night and we had some slight squalls. We do not go very fast today. We are out of the tropics and are more impatient as we near San Francisco. The changes of countenance occur with the change of wind and everyone is irritable in a

Mamma -

head wind *"as a matter of course."* This last expression is a favorite one
with our Hungarian and one he uses nearly twenty times a day.

Mamma is finishing a black *"mouslin de laine"* dress. We have all had
some arrowroot of Mamma's cooking in the aforesaid tin contrivance.
Mr. East is very much sunburnt. The thermometer is 69 degrees today,
being a difference of fifteen degrees in ten days.

The Captain's birthday, and he looks as if he wishes he had never had
a birthday.

<u>Friday October 8th.</u> Our pleasant anticipations are for awhile clouded,
for here, within ten degrees of San Francisco, we have calm or contrary
winds. Reports are about too, that the ship leaks more than even we
thought. The leaks had been stopped at Valparaiso, but the extreme heat
has expanded the seams of the ship. What alternations of hope and fear! It
seems as if our bright expectations—those we have so long and patiently
anticipated—would be blasted when near realization. It is indeed difficult
to keep up our spirits; the Captain, cross and pacing the deck with the spirit of one seeking whom he may devour—the passengers gloomy and discontented—while even Mr. Weisberger plays dominoes for hours to pass
away the time. I have just requested him to give the Captain the game, that
being I hope a means of restoring peace in some measure.

Yesterday a sail was seen from one of our masts but there is no sign of
a ship today. The weather is quite chilly now; we had a squall last night.
Oh, for a favorable wind to waft us to our desired haven. As I gaze on the
water frequently . . . it scarcely seems possible that there is any change

*from day to day. A few hours and our smooth sea is now troubled and tur-
bulent, wave dashes over wave, tossing the spray far around, and now
again all is hushed and tranquil and we sail softly on, as noiselessly as
though the monsters of this strange, watery waste might not hear.*

*October 8th [9th], Saturday. We are sailing along smoothly and slowly.
Mamma with Mr. East is on deck. I have finished a bag to hold her keys.*

*October 11th. We have had an unfavorable wind for several days and
yet we are within six hundred miles of San Francisco. Our vessel leaks
very much; three hundred gallons of water pumped out every hour.
When we sail fast we watch the compass and barometer and anxiously
inquire of everyone likely to know, how we are going and what prospect
we have of getting in. But all is vague and unsatisfactory. Indeed, we
have had much to depress us again, being within a few days sail and yet
no sign of the wind beyond a little swell to the westward. All our
patience is well-nigh exhausted with our resources; our work is finished,
our books read, and conversation worn out. Even preparing to land is
almost accomplished so that we can only sit down and think how nice it
would be if the wind would only change. One thing, we expect a very
rough time when it does.*

*The men are painting and cleaning ready for landing. We are rather
surprised occasionally now with the sight of a worm in our bread, biscuit, or potatoes, but we have fared well so long we cannot complain of
this. We have three or four fowls left. Our beef and soup, which is preserved in tins, is very good.*

Wednesday October 13th. Last night we had a splendid sunset again, though quite different to those I have mentioned before. It was very fiery indeed. The western heavens seemed as if in a blaze, tinging the surrounding clouds with red. This morning our wind died away and now our vessel is nearly heading towards San Francisco. Still we are over 560 miles off, and it seems as though we must always have another week before us. The time certainly hangs very heavily.

I exchanged a few words with Mrs. Waring today—the first in a long time. We spoke of the Valparaiso women and she told me she thought them like Indian women . . . She cannot speak without being vulgar.

We found today our dirty clothes were many of them spoiled from lying long and being damp. As many are new, this is a sad business.

Mr. John Waterson entertained us with the history of a most remarkable coat he wears, which always seems to me as if it were made for someone else, but he has given me a different idea now, particularly as he says he gave the man a good licking for making it too small!

We are now sailing well. Oh that it may last!

A pig killed today—a Chilean!

Mr. Waterson.

Thursday October 14th. Two ships in sight. Fair wind at last! Very rough, but Mr. Weisberger says always, "It is nothing."

Friday October 15th. Still going very fast. We are preparing our trunks for landing. We shall probably be at San Francisco by Sunday. It seems too delightful for realization: we are afraid to hope.

Ned, one of our little boys, the youngest on board, was guilty of a small theft, for which the Captain had him sit up on the spanker-boom astride with the word "Thief" on his back. He was left there until nearly four o'clock.

"Eclish, Caduash, Colobum, Nudzing Saratam Maggart." [These words, written in quotation marks without any explanation, are the phonetically spelled Hungarian words "Edes, Kedves Galambon, Nagyon Szeretem Magat"—which should be pronounced "Aydesh, kedvesh Gulumboe, nodyone seretem Mogat." It seems that on this day, Lucy asked Mr. Weisberger to speak to her in Hungarian, as she wished to hear how it sounded, whereupon he repeated the above words, which she recorded as best she could remember them. As he spoke he gave her a tender glance. Somewhat confused, she exclaimed, laughingly, "What dreadful-sounding words!" which was scarcely tactful, as he had just told her "My sweet, dear dove, I love you very much." Her response may account for his depression recorded the following day!—Ed.]

October 16th. This morning brings us more pleasure than any since we left New York. Land is descried from the masthead—Oh, what a joyful sound! Who can realize the delight with which these words strike on the ears of those who, for weeks and months have been tossed on the treacherous ocean, subject to the violence of the winds and waves? May this be our last voyage! And yet, what is before us? What may not the next few hours reveal? With what untold happiness shall we meet our beloved Papa, would all be well. Whatever may be our trials or vicissitudes, if this be the case we can combat them. And now should our hearts ascend in joyful praise to Him who has thus far brought us safely on our way.

Tomorrow we expect to land. All seem elated but Mr. Weisberger, who seems more than usually depressed—feeling as he does a stranger in a strange land.

<u>Sunday October 17th.</u> "Boast not thyself of tomorrow for thou knowest not what a day may bring forth."[20] We had confidently looked forward to landing this morning, but we strained our eyes vainly seeking the land, for the report of yesterday was false. However, we had a gentle breeze and before dinner the helmsman said, "There's land!" Although to an unpracticed eye naught could be seen but clouds above the horizon, a short time proved him right and once more did we rejoice at seeing land ourselves.

Gradually we neared the headlands of California, and the Golden Gate was pointed out to us as being the passage between a high cliff and some tall isolated rocks [The Farallon Islands—Ed.], that rose some ten or twelve miles from the mainland. Several ships were near us and two pilot boats were in sight. We were told that we would not get in until morning.

The evening proved to be foggy; we went to bed, our hearts beating high with expectation. About eleven o'clock a cannon was fired three times and lights hung out as a guide to the pilot—but in vain!—no pilot came to us.

Monday October 18th. A cold, foggy morning; not the least hope of landing. We are sadly disappointed. A vessel passed just before our bows this morning. The Captain is very much concerned; the fog is so dense we may be close to shore and yet he knows not which way to turn, in case during the night we have drifted inside those fearful rocks. He has, however, turned the ship's head to sea. We have just had a glimpse of our longed-for haven and now are to turn from it again. It is like showing food to a starving man and then taking it away; this seems hardest of all to bear.

Before night; the fog has dispersed enough to enable the Captain to see we are free of land. We have been sailing towards the sea some hours. Now the Captain has ordered the ship around again and during the night we shall sail gently towards shore.

Tuesday 19th. Early this morning we looked anxiously from our little window to see if the fog had left us; it had rained so hard in the night we hoped the atmosphere might be clear. But no—there it was—as thick as ever and although the sun shines brightly now and then, it seems to have but little effect. We are more and more dispirited.

Our vessel sailed within sound of the breakers last night and the Captain swears now he will not sail back, so we are again out to sea until the fog does clear off. This is an unknown coast, so any risk is a very dangerous experiment. Our lives might be saved did we run on the rocks, but our vessel would certainly go to pieces. It is a very trying predicament. Other ships are supposed to be near us. We may stand on and off for a week.

Envoy

What a change does a few hours effect in our feelings! Since dinner the fog has gradually dispersed and we are safe by the dreaded rocks. At half past five P.M. a pilot boat approached us; we watched it most anxiously. We saw it discharge a pilot at a neighboring vessel and then it came to us. One of the men, not a pilot but one who was familiar with the coast, then boarded us and we began to realize that our journey was at an end. This evening closes the voyage and with it my journal. Joys and sorrows, hopes and disappointments are the lot of human beings, but with my parting breath I would exclaim against a voyage around Cape Horn.

Our landing took place on the morning of the 20th of October, 1852—137 days at sea.

NOTES

1. Psalm 14:1.
2. Mother Carey's chickens is the common name for stormy petrels. Roger Tory Peterson, *A Field Guide to Western Birds* (Boston: Houghton Mifflin Co., 1941).
3. The three books Lucy mentions are as follows: *Uncle Tom's Cabin*, an anti-slavery novel by Harriet Beecher Stowe; *Queechy* by Elizabeth Wetherall, a pseudonym for Susan Warner; and *Ivanhoe,* by Sir Walter Scott.
4. Joseph Addison was an English essayist and poet. *The Campaign* won him recognition.
5. In the mid-nineteenth century an eyestone—a tiny portion from a particular seashell—was used to remove a foreign substance from the eye. The eyestone was placed in the inner corner of the eye under the lid and as it worked its way out at the outside corner it would sometimes bring the foreign substance with it.
6. Juan Fernandez consists of two islands four hundred miles west of Valparaiso. Associated with Robinson Crusoe and his island adventure, it was also known as a penal colony.
7. The Rio de la Plata is an estuary of the Uruguay River that separates Argentina and Brazil. It is a major waterway of the western hemisphere.
8. "Doubling the Cape" was considered the most dangerous part of the voyage. Cape Horn experiences particularly strong storms due to its position between the Atlantic and Pacific Oceans. The oceans, with their currents and winds, meet in a most violent manner and many ships were lost or badly damaged in "rounding the Horn."
9. See Richard Henry Dana's *Two Years Before the Mast* for an exposé of abuse at sea.
10. Lucy was correct that Cape Horn is 56°S; however, the Cape of Good Hope is actually closer to 34°S.
11. Valparaiso is the second-largest city and harbor in central Chile. Talcahuano is two hundred miles south of Valparaiso.
12. The Cordilleras is the mountain system running from Tierra del Fuego and the Falkland Islands north between Chile and Argentina to Venezuela, and is only slightly less lofty than the Himalayas. Current usage calls these the Andes.
13. The *Rariton* is a 79-ton schooner built in 1837 at Crosswick Creek, N.J. *List of American-flag Merchant Vessels, 1769–1867,* comp. Forrest R. Holdcamper (Washington, D.C.: U.S. National Archives and Records Service, General Services Administration, 1968).
14. Although the Mexican-American War was over in 1848, feelings on both sides still ran high.
15. A gowney is a booby gannet. See Peterson, *A Field Guide to Western Birds*, p. 15.
16. Webster defines a tract as "a propagandizing pamphlet, especially one on a religious or political subject."
17. This is probably the great frigatebird or white-tailed tropicbird. Both of these have two tail feathers that look like one. Peterson, pp. 259–61.
18. This is probably the brown booby or the blue-faced booby. Ibid., p. 260.
19. The *Witch of the Wave* was an 87-ton schooner built in Essex, Connecticut. See *List of American-flag Merchant Vessels, 1769–1867*.
20. Proverbs 27:1.

LATER YEARS

An unusual view of San Francisco from a high point on the south side, 1850. It shows Yerba Buena Cove (which is now filled in), the central wharf, and in the distance the Marin shore and Mt. Tamalpais.

San Francisco had already seen quite a change in the two years between its founding in 1847 and the arrival of Joseph Kendall in 1849. The sleepy pueblo of Yerba Buena had its name changed to San Francisco in 1847. Its population dropped by more than half in 1848 as the news of gold spread through the streets. Nearly all the men and boys stampeded for the goldfields. Thousands more arrived through the Golden Gate and Joseph Kendall was on the crest of that wave.

This influx was mostly of hardworking honest folk, and crime was not much of a problem. But if San Francisco in 1848 had seen a great exodus to the mine fields, it also saw great growth in the early fifties. Many of the miners, disillusioned with the slim pickings, the weather, and disease, drifted back to the city, finding a "living" as best they could. Jobs were not hard to find for those who wanted to work, but not all sought "honest" labor, and crime grew to such a volume in 1851 that a Vigilante Committee took law into its own hands, meting out justice much like many a western frontier town.[1] It must have been after the Committee had rid the city of most of the criminal element that Joseph, in coming to San Francisco from Stockton, thought that his wife and daughters could now come to him, "as it was getting more civilized," having more women than formerly, "and churches, too."

Joseph Kendall opened a shop while he waited for the arrival of his family. He advertised as a "sign" painter[2] which was known to mean that he painted houses and their interiors as well as commercial establishments. There was plenty of room for sign painters in San Francisco, especially after the devastating fire of May 8, 1851.

The *Josephine* was met by Joseph Kendall, who was delighted to see his family after three-and-one-half years of separation. Lucy's small upright piano, an unusual sight in those days, drew quite a crowd when it was delivered from the docks. Finally, the family and baggage, Annie's canaries included, were bundled into a carriage, and all set off for a little house on Yerba Buena Street at the foot of what was to become Nob Hill. Joseph had it all in readiness even to the curtains in the windows and pincushions on the bureaus; the one in Annie's room had her name spelled in pins on the top.

Shortly after their arrival, Lucy and Annie opened a school because they wanted pocket money of their own. In "The Misses Kendalls' School for Young Ladies" held in the Methodist Episcopal Church on Powell Street, the young ladies taught first-, second-, and third-grade classes, and lessons in pianoforte, drawing, and French. It was so unusual to hear piano music in those early days that passersby used to stop and listen.

Saturdays often found Lucy and Annie riding sidesaddle (at $5.00 an afternoon) through the sand dunes to the beach. Charlotte Kendall, considered a fine horsewoman, accompanied them when opportunity presented itself. Among the friends who joined them was William Herrick, an adventurous young man newly arrived from New Hampshire on the ship *Westward Ho*.[3] William's interest in Lucy was evidenced by the inscriptions in several books he gave to her. Although Charlotte considered books "proper" and acceptable gifts for young ladies, she did not approve of

William Herrick from a daguerreotype taken in the early 1850s.

Pencil sketch by Joseph Kendall, 1849. This church is believed to be the first Protestant church in California. It was constructed from "Oregon scantling," with a roof made from ship's sails, and walls and ceiling from cotton cloth.

William. She may not have seen the five years he spent at sea as a teenager and his desire to be an pursue a career as an engraver as much of a future for her beloved daughter

In 1854, only one-and-one-half years after arriving in San Francisco, Charlotte Kendall suffered a fall from which she was never to recover. On her deathbed she made Lucy promise that she would never marry William Herrick. When Jonas Paxton heard of his sister's death, he wrote to Joseph Kendall encouraging the family to come home to England. In a letter, to Lucy on June 29, 1854, he repeated his plea:

. . . I have heard of a little of a Mr. Herrick and I respect his character because he has loved you. But dear darling Lucy, pause in this great matter and let us all see you and hear all connected with it. I feel assured your precious, sainted mother has good reasons for her objections or she would not have raised them. Come to us, my child, and may God protect you all. . . .

But Lucy, who no doubt respected her uncle's wishes, had vowed never to go to sea again under any circumstances and she was never to see the Paxton family again. A few months later, Annie Kendall, then just eighteen, was married to Albert Miller in San Francisco. Time passed and on January 1, 1856, in spite of her mother's last wish, Lucy and William Herrick were married in Joseph Kendall's house. A few months after the wedding, Lucy wrote the following letter to her new mother-in-law in New Hampshire.

123

San Francisco, July 18th, 1856

My dear Mother,

I have been thinking for some time I would write a letter to you. My dear husband has long wished me to do so, but I always felt a little timid about the first letter until I received so many kind and tender messages from you, placing me at once in your heart and interest as a daughter and the wife of your beloved William. How often when watching the countenance of my husband, as he eagerly and joyously has been reading a letter from "Mother," has a pain thrilled through me at the thought that not long since I, too, had a fond mother, whose words came full of love to encourage and cheer me in every event of life. But those lips are silent, never more to be heard on earth; and how often while wiping away the tears has my William promised me that his mother would love me, and that I should share with him her affection. And I have lately felt that though personally unknown to you I am doing so, and it has been a source of much happiness to me.

When a gentleman marries of course new ties and new interests claim his attention, but with William nothing has drawn him from the love of mother and home. Scarcely a day passes without his speaking of you or his father. I know you all so well; your housekeeping and skill with the needle; Father's fruit trees and farming, and how much his daughters (in-law) love him; then all about Moses and Henry and their wives and children, until I can follow my dear husband in thought among you all.

It is true that we have been married but a short time but our acquaintance has been a long one, and we have learned to mingle our hopes and fears, joys and sorrows together. Even in this short time we have had some disappointments and some trials, but oh how greatly are they lessened by the confidence and sympathy which we both possess in and for each other, and by the thought that we are together, aiming to live for that life which is eternal.

My health is not as robust as I could wish, and my spirits suffer sometimes. But William is so patient and even and soothing, I feel how very much we have to be thankful for—a nice sweet home, with plenty of loving friends, and hearts full of love for each other.

William works very hard at engraving and has often much to try him in a pecuniary way, but we live as economically as we can, and he has the gift for looking at the bright side, whenever there is one, so that we are not often much depressed.

My father lives with us, and my only sister with her husband and child live next door. We are very happy all together. I wonder if we shall ever meet. William wants to send you my daguerreotype, but I do not like to stand the test of such an introduction. Nevertheless, I suppose he will have his own way in this some day. I would rather offer you and his dear father a heart full of love for the parents of my beloved husband, and be estimed by that.

Will you write me a long letter? I thank you for the recipes. I am not very clever about cooking, I consider it one of my principal weaknesses, but William seems satisfied with everything I do, and this encourages me to persevere.

I am expecting him home shortly to lunch. He comes a considerable distance, but it pleases me to see him once during the long day. I wish I could tell you something to interest you, but my chief end in writing will be attained if I succeed in convincing you that you have, in California, an affectionate daughter.

Lucy F. Herrick

Please give much love to father and brothers. I never had a brother until William gave me his, with the exception of my sister's husband. There is a dear Grandmother, too, at Haverhill, that I wish to be kindly remembered to. All William's relatives are dear to me.

After her marriage, Lucy's life was taken up with family matters; she bore nine children in the years from 1856 to 1872. Annie and Albert Miller shared a double house on Sacramento Street with the Herricks, Joseph Kendall, and Uncle Harry East. The families spent time together in an "apartment," or sitting room, between the two sides of the house. Annie and Lucy would wait in the apartment for the return of their husbands on "steamer nights"[4] when the mail steamship docked.

In the late 1850s Joseph Kendall became a helpless invalid after a stroke and died in 1864. William Herrick pursued careers as a commercial engraver and newspaperman, and then his daily occupation shifted to the commercial world of accounting, life insurance, and real estate. This allowed him greater freedom to follow his interest in art, ships, and the sea. With William's small income and nine children to raise, it took planning to manage the household. Somehow, Lucy coped. When funds were low she gave piano lessons or painted watercolors. Her home was a friendly place with books, flowers, and music. Her housekeeping, however, was always casual, and she never liked to cook. Always cheerful under difficult circumstances, Lucy practiced patience and gentleness which sustained her family and enabled them to surmount any adversity they encountered.

We have come to the end of Lucy's story gleaned from diaries, letters, and family legend. She lived through the coming of gas and electric light, the telegraph, the telephone, indoor plumbing, and the horseless carriage. She traveled to California on a long and dangerous voyage around Cape Horn, then saw that mode of travel replaced by the the transcontinental railroad. While Lucy and William raised their children they helped build San Francisco from a rugged frontier town to a center of the western United States. Lucy died in June, 1906, at age 78. William followed her in September.[5]

Lucy and William Herrick drawn by their daughter Margaret in 1902.

NOTES

1. Andrew Rolle, *California, A History*, 3rd ed. (Arlington Heights, Ill.: AHM Publishing Co., 1978), pp. 228–31.
2. San Francisco Business Directory of 1852.
3. *Westward Ho* was one of the clipper ships in the clipper-ship derby.
4. Bret Harte wrote, "Indeed at that time San Francisco may have been said to have lived from steamer day to steamer day; bills were made due on that date, interest computed to that period, and accounts settled. The next day was the turning of a new leaf: another essay to fortune, another inspiration of energy. So recognized was the fact that even ordinary changes of condition, social and domestic, were put aside until after steamer day. 'I'll see what I can do after steamer day' was the common cautious or hopeful formula."
5. Lucy and William were interred in the Herrick plot in the Oakland Cemetery next to Lucy's parents and two sons and two daughters who predeceased them.

BIBLIOGRAPHY

Barry, T. A., and B. A. Patten. *Men and Memories of San Francisco in the "Spring of 50."* San Francisco: A. L. Bancroft & Co., 1873.

Bean, Walton. *California: An Interpretive History.* New York: McGraw-Hill Book Co., 1968.

Colton, Rev. Walter, USN. *Three Years in California.* New York: A. S. Barnes & Co., 1850.

Cutler, Carl C. *Greyhounds of the Sea: The Story of the American Clipper Ship.* New York: Halcyon House, 1930.

Dana, Richard Henry. *Two Years Before the Mast.* New York: Harper & Son, 1841.

Gordon, John D., III. *Authorized by No Law: San Francisco Committee of Vigilance of 1856.* Pasadena, Calif.: United States Circuit Court for the District of California, 9th Circuit Historical Society, 1987.

Holdcamper, Forrest R., comp. *New York Register of Vessels,* Washington, D.C.: U.S. National Archives and Record Service, General Services Administration, 1968.

Hughs, Edan Milton. *Artists in California 1786–1940.* San Francisco: Hughs Publishing Co., 1989.

Hughs, Thomas. *Tom Brown's School Days.* Cambridge, Mass.: Macmillan & Co., 1857.

Kendall, Joseph. *A Landsman's Journey to California . . . An Account of the Voyage 'Round the Horn of the Bark* Canton. San Francisco: Taylor & Taylor, 1935.

Nelson's Pictorial Guide—Books for Tourists: The Isle of Wight. London, Edinburgh, and New York: T. Nelson & Sons, n.d.

New York City Directories. 1837, 1850, 1851, 1852.

Pomfret, John E., ed. *California Gold Rush Voyages, 1848–1849: Three Original Narratives.* Westport, Conn.: Greenwood Press, 1954.

Rolle, Andrew. *California, A History.* 3rd ed. Arlington Heights, Ill.: AHM Publishing Corp., 1978.

Russell, Amy R. "The Early Years of William Francis Herrick." *California Historical Society Quarterly* 26, no. 3 (September 1947).

Rydell, Raymond A. *Cape Horn to the Pacific.* Berkeley and Los Angeles: University of California Press, 1952.

San Francisco City Directory. San Francisco: Morgan, A. W. & Co., 1852, 1858.

San Francisco City Directory. San Francisco: Harris Bogardus & Labott, 1856.

INDEX

Voyage to California: Written at Sea, 1852

Designed by Kathleen Thorne-Thomsen
in Souvenir with Optima heads
Copy edited by Guilland Sutherland and Sherri Schottlaender
Printed by McNaughton & Gunn
on Writers Offset Natural with Rainbow endpapers